Judgment Obtained By Fraud

how Peninsula helped fool an Employment Tribunal

Foreword

We open this book with a message from the Claimant

"Peninsula,
threats only work when
the person you're threatening
has something of value to lose.

In my case, that was my job
and my career, which you
already helped take away!"

Introduction

This book deals with Employment Tribunal Case No. 2405443/2015, *'Mr J Bagnall v KS Hotels Ltd ('Leigh Hotels Ltd' at time of publication)'*, Company No. 08897530; herein referred to as the *'Employer'*.

The Employer *(Respondent)* was taken to an Employment Tribunal *(ET)* which was heard by Judge Horne in Manchester 2016. The Employer was represented by Peninsula Business Services *(now Peninsula)*; herein referred to as *'Peninsula'*.

The issue was originally one of *'Employment Law'* i.e. the unfair dismissal of the Claimant *(employee)* by the Employer. The Claimant worked the night shift in the Employer's only hotel at the time.

The issue evolved into a different branch of law when the Employer secured the ET judgment in their favour by knowingly giving false written and verbal statements i.e. they *'obtained a Judgment by fraud'*.

It's only due to evidence and revelations coming to light months after the ET that it can now be demonstrated those written and verbal statements were false and that the Employer, with the full backing of Peninsula, was guilty of a conscious and deliberate dishonesty in the presentation and pursuit of their defence i.e. the judgment was obtained by the Employer's fraud and that Peninsula was a knowing and willing party to that fraud.

The evidence and revelations were very relevant to the

issues to be decided at the Employment Tribunal yet, they were missing from Employer's ET3 response statement, missing from Employer's witness statements, missing from Employer's disclosed documents, and missing from Employer's verbal evidence to the ET.

The bulk of the evidence was not disclosed to Claimant despite him making a Subject Access Request in 2015 and a subsequent complaint to the Information Commissioner's Office *(ICO)*. The evidence is mostly in the form of internal written communications, about the Claimant, made between Employer and Peninsula during 2014 and 2015. As the communications related to an identified or identifiable person, namely the Claimant, it became his personal data and ought to have been disclosed as part of a Subject Access Request. However, Peninsula/Employer stated to the ICO that the communications contained *'advice in connection with possible litigation'*; thereby convincing the ICO that the communications were protected by Legal Professional Privilege *(LPP)*.

It's difficult to see how the ICO accepted this reason from Peninsula/Employer, and sided with them on the issue, as there were no legal proceedings ongoing or anticipated when the communications were made. While a disciplinary could be used as evidence in, or be the cause of, legal proceedings further down the line, holding a disciplinary does not constitute legal proceedings taking place, nor does it guarantee that legal proceedings will ever take place. The dominant purpose for the communications in this instance was to discuss the Claimant's respective disciplinary hearings at the time. Further, the communications themselves did NOT contain Legal Advice; giving legal advice was a reserved activity and only communications between trading Solicitors and Barristers and their clients were subject to such privilege. Peninsula was not trading as Solicitors or Barristers; Peninsula was trading as advisors and were NOT authorised to give legal advice because they were NOT regulated by the Solicitors Regulation Authority *(SRA)*.

It was also clarified by the Supreme Court in *'Prudential plc v Special Commissioner of Income Tax'*, prior to Claimant contacting the ICO, that LPP only applied to advice given by Lawyers and did not extend to advice given by people outside the legal profession. The ICO themselves held the position that, regardless of what the person giving the advice is qualified in, if that person is not employed as a lawyer then no lawyer-client relationship can arise and any advice they give is not covered by LPP; yet, when dealing with the Claimant, the ICO determined that, despite Peninsula NOT being employed as lawyers, the communications were covered by LPP simply because of Peninsula's involvement.

The evidence was not disclosed to the Employment Tribunal either despite a Disclosure Order being in place for *'not just those documents upon which they relied but also those documents which were relevant'*. The evidence in this book was very relevant and, had it been disclosed at the time, would have materially changed the cross examination of the Employer's witnesses and completely changed the outcome of the Tribunal; in fact, Peninsula/Employer would likely have negotiated a settlement before any Employment Tribunal.

Peninsula/Employer didn't simply withhold relevant documents at ET; they had a reckless disregard for the truth and knowingly put false information in their place. This, in turn, denied Claimant a fair hearing.

Background Information

The reason for doing this book is that Employment Law only gives you a very short window of 42 days to appeal an ET decision; it may be extended if the Court grants permission, but that's a very big 'IF'. The evidence we now have came into our possession over 12 months after the ET decision; well outside the 42 day window. It was then a slow process to cross reference all the material from the disciplinary hearings and the Employment Tribunal with the new evidence in order to put a case together.

We may be out of time to have a Court of Law hold Peninsula and Employer accountable for their actions, but we can still put the information out there which will allow the public to make a more informed choice on whether or not they want to use the services of these companies.

(The identities and positions of some parties have not been anonymized as they are already a matter of public record for all to see).

May 2009 - Claimant started his employment as a Night Porter in a branded hotel. His main tasks were cleaning and resetting meeting rooms; this was a non-management position with no managerial responsibilities. Only the basic online Fire Safety and First Aid training was a legal mandatory requirement for ALL staff regardless of position. The operational structure in place was separate departments with their own department managers, and dedicated staff covering just their own department. The Night Porter role was tagged on to the Front Office department for payroll purposes; the Claimant didn't do any reception work at all.

Nov 2013 - Claimant became Night Supervisor within the Front Office department by responding to an internal job advert and partaking in a formal selection process to determine his suitability for the role. The Supervisor role carried some new responsibilities such as admin, night rota, and reception work; all of which training was provided for. The role did not require any additional First Aid or Fire Safety training and the hotel was regularly left without any Manager on site during Claimant's shift.

June 2014 - the hotel was acquired by the Employer, KS Hotels Ltd; a company in the same business sector but unconnected to the previous owners or brand. A new General Manager was appointed to run the hotel for the Employer *(we'll call her 'Miss GM')*; existing hotel staff either quit or were TUPEd over to the Employer. The previous branding was removed and the hotel remained unbranded until Oct 2014; during that time the Employer ran the hotel under the rules and procedures that were already in place prior to TUPE from the previous owners.

July 2014 - a temporary General Manager *(Mr Frodsham)* was appointed after Miss GM suddenly resigned and walked out. On 30 July Mr Frodsham sent an internal memo to ALL staff advertising the roles of Guest Service Managers *(GSM)*. GSM was NOT a KS Hotels designation; it was an InterContinental Hotels Group *(IHG)* designation and the jobs were advertised in preparation for the oncoming rebrand of the hotel as part of an IHG franchise agreement.

Aug 2014 - Mr Brimacombe was appointed as Deputy General Manager, a position that had not existed under the previous owners. On 08 Aug Mr Brimacombe sent an internal memo to ALL staff reminding them about the GSM roles and provided a cut-off date for applications. Claimant subsequently applied for the role of Guest Service Manager for the night shift. On 21 – 23 Aug Claimant and a selection of staff took part in *'First Aid at Work'* training; this was NOT legally required mandatory training, it was simply additional internal training which was required by the IHG franchise agreement. A certificate of completion was ONLY issued if you met the standard by passing an assessment test at the end of the course.

Sept 2014 - Peninsula conducted a Fire Risk Assessment of the hotel on 05 Sept in preparation for the rebranding to an IHG property.

Oct 2014 - the hotel was officially rebranded to a Holiday Inn Express on 01 Oct 2014. All departments merged into one and all staff now worked most areas of the hotel rather than just one of multiple departments.

On that same day, Mr Frodsham appointed Claimant as a Guest Service Manager in response to Claimant's application for the role; this was a more senior position than Claimant currently held and one which had not existed under the previous owners OR with the Employer themselves. Guest Service Manager was an IHG designation and was introduced as part of the rebranding to an IHG franchise hotel. No selection process was conducted by Employer to determine Claimant's suitability for the role; Claimant was simply told by Mr Frodsham that he was now a GSM, but was never informed what his duties and responsibilities were as a GSM.

Nor was Claimant informed of any changes to Fire Safety procedures which, had there been any changes, it was a legal requirement on Employer's part to inform their staff and have each member of staff sign off that they had been informed; this in turn meant Claimant was still operating under the pre-IHG procedures which didn't require any *'advanced'* training. Claimant was never instructed to view specific information contained on the IHG intranet *(the intranet was just a reference tool and so vast that, unless directed to specific parts, it would be unreasonable to expect anyone to read through it all)*.

The method used by Employer in appointing staff to the more senior roles of GSM was not based on management experience or training; this is demonstrated by the fact that two receptionists in non-managerial roles, with no managerial training or experience within the hotel, skipped the Trainee GSM role and were appointed to full GSM positions while, at the same time, one existing Supervisor with years of supervisory experience within the hotel was only given the position of Trainee GSM.

Near the end of Oct 2014 Claimant made a private Facebook post, to his group of 10 friends, regarding an incident at work; this was brought to the attention of Mr Brimacombe and Mr Frodsham by another GSM *(we'll call her 'Miss Snitch')* who was friends with Claimant on Facebook.

Nov 2014 - Claimant was called to a Disciplinary Hearing for the Facebook post he made in Oct. While Employer's initial concerns were credible, and warranted an investigation, their conclusions that the post HAD *'damaged the business'* and *'brought the company into disrepute'* were not credible as they were not supported by any investigation. In fact, the notes of the meeting held with Claimant demonstrate that the Facebook post was unlikely to have caused any genuine damage to the business as it was private, accessible to a handful of people, did not name the hotel or brand, did not disclose any personal information or identify the guest concerned, and was only visible for a few hours.

Because the post was private, Claimant's Facebook security measures had to be circumvented in order for Employer to obtain the evidence i.e. Employer requested that Miss Snitch take a screenshot and pass it on to them; which she did.

Further, *'damage to the business'* and *'bringing the company into disrepute'* were NEVER investigated or established; therefore, in this instance, the post did not meet the requirements of Serious or Gross Misconduct as set out by Employer's own Disciplinary Procedures. Nonetheless, the Employer issued Claimant with a *'First & Final Written Warning'* for Serious Misconduct by relying on hypotheticals rather than investigating and establishing the actual *'facts'*; this was contrary to Disciplinary Procedures which demanded that facts be *'carefully'* investigated before any disciplinary action is taken.

The whole experience made Claimant ill and he had some time off sick. While off, the Claimant was diagnosed as suffering from work related stress; a common mental health issue but one Claimant never had prior to Employer taking over the hotel. The Employer was made aware of the diagnosis.

Dec 2014 - Claimant informed Employer that he had been diagnosed with extremely high blood pressure and was now on medication; very concerning for a 47 year old and another condition that Claimant never had prior to Employer taking over the hotel. Claimant also informed Employer that his health condition could affect his ability to carry out day-to-day activities i.e. a potential disability; Clamant suggested that an Occupational Health Assessment be conducted.

Jan 2015 - Employer conducted a *'Workplace Stress Assessment'* at the beginning of Claimant's shift on 01 Jan and assessed Claimant as showing signs of stress; a condition known to affect decision making and one which Employer knew Claimant had suffered from since Nov 2014. Employer concluded the assessment by agreeing to meet with Claimant fortnightly to monitor the situation; however, no further meetings ever took place.

After assessing Claimant as showing signs of stress, the Employer never asked Claimant if he was fit to carry on with his shift that night; but asking someone with impaired decision making to make a *'decision'* on their ability to carry on, would be like asking a drunk if they are fit to drive. Nor did Employer seek professional medical advice to determine if Claimant was fit to carry on with his shift; instead, Employer left Claimant alone and unsupported, in charge of an occupied hotel, knowing he could be called upon to make management decisions at any time, such as those regarding *'Health & Safety'*, and knowing they had just assessed him as essentially being unfit to make such decisions.

It was during that very shift when Miss Snitch, the next GSM on duty, phoned in sick. Claimant had to make a decision regarding cover staff for Miss Snitch's absence. It was part of Claimant's job to make such decisions but, no procedures were in place for Claimant to follow, no restrictions were placed on any staff which prevented them from being used as cover, the only guidance regarding cover staff was contained in the Employee Handbook which stated it was an *'Express Condition'* and *'essential for operational efficiency'* that staff can be called upon to take over duties *'performed by colleagues'*, and Claimant NEVER had prior experience of dealing with a Manager absence; Claimant was simply left on his own, unsupported, while suffering from stress when the issue arose.

There were written procedures in place for Miss Snitch to follow i.e. SHE had to personally report HER absence directly to HER Line Manager *(Mr Brimacombe/Mr Frodsham)* at the earliest possible opportunity; but it was later revealed she failed to comply with those procedures and contacted the Claimant instead. Employer deemed it as acceptable for Miss Snitch not to have followed her Management procedures citing that *'it was much more sensible'* for Miss Snitch to telephone the Claimant as he was on duty in the hotel.

However, given that Mr Frodsham stated he and Mr Brimacombe were *'on call'* through the night, together with the fact there were no written exceptions concerning issues that occurred at night, Employer's reasoning made a mockery of those procedures; the 24 hour nature of the business was built into the procedures as demonstrated by having Mr Brimacombe and Mr Frodsham on call, which allowed them as Line Manager to be notified directly.

Claimant did send an email to Mr Frodsham at the time

informing him of the absence, but only to let Mr Frodsham know that Claimant had been made aware of it; the email was NOT intended to be the primary source of information regarding the absence because it was reasonable of Claimant to believe that Miss Snitch, as a Manager, had followed her procedures and personally informed Mr Brimacombe/Mr Frodsham herself.

Claimant then made a judgement call and decided to leave non-management staff in charge of the hotel i.e. the Chef, a Guest Service Assistant, and a Pot Washer. Claimant's decision was based on HIS knowledge and HIS experience within the hotel i.e. Claimant KNEW AS FACT there was not always a Manager on site *(he worked 4 years in a non-Manager role with no 'advanced fire safety training' and had experience of there being no Manager on site)*, Claimant BELIEVED the other Night staff were NOT Managers and that Employer sometimes left them without a Manager on site *(which the other Night Staff confirmed to Claimant as being true during the Disciplinary adjournment but, they did not want to be witnesses for Claimant due to fear of losing their jobs)*, Claimant BELIEVED the other Night Staff had only done the same basic Fire Safety training that he had done *(it was only at ET that Employer disclosed the other Night Staff had done additional fire safety training on Claimant's night off, thereby establishing why Claimant had no knowledge of it)*, Claimant BELIEVED the Chef to be a *'Responsible Person'* because the Chef was left unmanaged and in charge of the kitchen at the time which is the most dangerous place in the hotel, and because the Chef had previously held a Supervisory position prior to transferring into the kitchen.

On 29 Jan, during a Disciplinary Hearing, Employer swiftly

disregarded all of Claimant's reasoning and, in doing so, failed to acknowledge that there was a gap in their procedures, in their training, or in Claimant's understanding of the GSM role. Claimant even stated at the Disciplinary Hearing that *'this is clearly a development issue which you have turned into a conduct issue'*, but Employer failed to engage with that possibility. Instead, Employer judged Claimant on what THEY maintained he *'ought to have known'* rather than on what Claimant was telling them he knew.

Despite having the option of demoting Claimant to a lesser role, the Employer chose to dismiss him simply because the 2014 warning was still live on his file; and they had to rely on that live warning to justify dismissal because Claimant's actions in this instance were NOT Gross Misconduct. Again, the Employer sanctioned Claimant by relying on hypotheticals rather than investigating and establishing the actual *'facts'* on which THEY relied; this was contrary to Disciplinary Procedures which demanded that facts be *'carefully'* investigated before any disciplinary action is taken.

Claimant raised his *'work related stress'* during the Disciplinary Process but did not rely on it directly as mitigation for his actions; but then Claimant believed his actions were reasonable based on his own knowledge. It did not occur to Claimant that the *'work related stress'* may have affected his decision making on the night in question, or may have affected how he perceived his own experience within the hotel, or may even have affected how he defended against the Disciplinary allegations.

The Employer, however, had no such medical condition affecting their judgment, had full knowledge of Claimant's condition, were fully aware it could be a potential disability, had noted Claimant's demeanor months prior to and during the Disciplinary Hearing, and had a *'Duty of Care'* to the Claimant; therefore, Employer ought to have taken the *'work related stress'* into account without the need for Claimant to prompt them, especially as Claimant's decision occurred just a few hours after Employer assessed him as showing signs of stress which affects decision making.

This book is not a critique of Claimant's conduct; whatever that conduct may have been, Claimant was still entitled to a fair hearing which meant not being pre-judged, the sanction not being pre-determined and the Disciplinary/Appeal Officers being impartial. With the help of evidence that Peninsula/Employer withheld from the Employment Tribunal, this book demonstrates that all those basic rights were denied to the Claimant with the approval of Peninsula, and that Peninsula/Employer went on to mislead the ET.

Frauds committed by Peninsula/Employer

The frauds committed at Employment Tribunal were a true testament of Peninsula's and the Employer's character i.e. they were dishonest, had no integrity, and showed utter contempt for the Court.

While some of the frauds may seem insignificant on their own, they were used to support other frauds. Collectively they all had an enormous negative impact on the fairness of the Employment Tribunal. If all fraudulent statements put forward by Peninsula/Employer were removed, and all the genuine evidence was disclosed as it ought to have been, judgment could only have fallen in favour of the Claimant.

For easy reference we have numbered the frauds.

1. **Employer put to Employment Tribunal that Claimant HAD an expired warning on file from the previous owners of the hotel, a warning they claim not to have taken into account because *'KS Hotels taking over was a fresh start and employees were entitled to the benefit of the doubt'* (see *'Image 001'*); which begs the question, if it wasn't taken into account, why mention it to the Tribunal?** – However, that was a conscious and deliberate dishonesty as Claimant had never been given any warnings by the previous owners; no such warning was documented in Claimant's personnel file which Employer disclosed to Claimant as part of a Subject Access Request in 2015, and Employer themselves failed to

disclose any supporting documents of this alleged warning to the Employment Tribunal, documents that would have existed had a warning by the previous owners been issued.

Employer put this false narrative forward to Employment Tribunal as a clear attempt to taint the Claimant's character and discredit him from the outset by defining that he was a problem employee even before Employer took over the business.

Image 001

> I had seen that James had been given a warning previously, but this had expired in February 2014.
>
> As it had expired, I didn't pay any attention to it. My view was that KS Hotels taking over was a fresh start and employees were entitled to the benefit of the doubt.

From Mr Frodsham's written statement of 'FACT' to the Employment Tribunal – Mr Frodsham falsely states that Claimant had been given a warning by the previous owners.

2. **Employer put to Employment Tribunal, or inferred, that the job title of *'Supervisor'* simply changed to *'Guest Service Manager'* under new *'IHG terminology'* brought in as a result of the hotel rebrand *(see 'Image 002a' and 'Image 002b')*; thereby establishing that both Manager and Supervisor were the same position and that Claimant had been a *'Manager'* for over 12 months** - however, undisclosed evidence *(see 'Image 002c')* demonstrates that this was a conscious and deliberate dishonesty as all GSM positions were advertised internally and Claimant had to apply for the role; therefore the job title did not simply change from one to the other. Had Claimant not applied for

the role of Night GSM he would have remained in the lower position of Supervisor.

A revelation also came to light, months after the ET, that the Employer had appointed a member of Night Staff to the position of Night Supervisor *(Claimant's job title prior to the rebrand)* in 2015 around the same time as appointing a new Guest Service Manager to replace Claimant; which further demonstrates that the role of *'Supervisor'* still existed, that it was a separate role to that of a GSM, that both roles were of different seniority and would therefore have different levels of duties and responsibilities associated with them *(now very relevant to fraud 3)*.

Claimant's *'Supervisor'* role did not guarantee that he was suitable for the more senior role of Guest Service Manager; suitability for any role would normally be determined by a formal selection process, a process the previous owners carried out before appointing Claimant to the Supervisor role, but which Employer failed to carry out when appointing Claimant to the more senior position of GSM.

Image 002a

> the terminology changed to 'guest services manager' and '- assistant'

From Mr Brimacombe's written statement of 'FACT' to the Employment Tribunal in relation to job titles after the rebranding of the hotel. Mr Brimacombe states that job titles simply changed because of new IHG terminology i.e. Supervisor changed to Guest Service Manager, Receptionist also changed to Guest Service Manager, and everyone else became a Guest Service Assistant (GSA). Curiously, Mr Brimacombe didn't explain how, if the new terminology changed job titles from one to another, an existing Supervisor became a Trainee GSM, or how two other Receptionist became GSAs at the same time the job title changed to GSM, or that there was still a Supervisor role despite the new terminology supposedly renaming the Supervisor role to GSM.

Image 002b

> As part of the rebrand to Holiday Inn Express in October 2014, the new 'structure' referred to this positions as 'guest services manager'.

From Mr Frodsham's written statement of 'FACT' to the Employment Tribunal – Mr Frodsham, who admitted to reading Mr Brimacombe's statement before writing his own, conveniently backs up Mr Brimacombe by stating the job title of Supervisor simply changed to 'guest services manager'. Curiously, Mr Frodsham also failed to disclose that there was still a Supervisor role despite the new terminology supposedly renaming the Supervisor role to Guest Service Manager.

Image 002c

> **To:** The Team
> **From:** Charlie
> **CC:** Steven Frodsham
> **Date:** 15/08/2014
> **Re:** GSM Applications
>
> ---
>
> Hi
>
> Following on from Stevens MEMO on the 30th July regarding the applications for GSM roles (guest service Managers) within the hotel, the cut off date for applications is the 22nd August 2014 at midday.
>
> If interested please let me know with a full CV by 22nd AUGUST 2014
>
> Thanks
> Charlie

Internal memo, from Mr Brimacombe, confirming that GSM roles were advertised in a previous memo from Mr Frodsham.

If job titles simply changed names, due to 'new terminology', there would have been no need to advertise for GSMs as they would already exist due to the 'new terminology' i.e. existing Supervisors would be called GSMs. The reason the Guest Service Manager jobs were advertised, and Claimant had to apply for one of the positions, is because Employer had no existing 'like with like' roles; Guest Service Managers were totally NEW roles and MORE SENIOR than the positions held by any of the current staff the jobs were aimed at.

3. **Employer put to Employment Tribunal, or inferred, that Claimant was a *'Highly Experienced Manager'*; Judge Horne relied on this when making his decision** *(see 'Image 003a')* – however, this was a conscious and deliberate dishonesty as Claimant had only been a *'Manager'* for 3 months *(that's 12 weeks of which 2 weeks Claimant was off sick, and 1 week Claimant was on holiday)*; while Claimant gained some experience as a *'Manager'* in that small amount of time, it fell extremely short of him being *'Highly Experienced'* as a *'Manager'*.

Employer needed the Tribunal to believe that Claimant was *'highly experienced'* as a *'Manager'* in order to negate the fact they could not provide any paper trail to support that Claimant had done the *'advanced'* fire training which they relied on to dismiss him, and to negate the fact they had NOT made Claimant aware of specific conditions, procedures and rules which they also relied on to dismiss him *(see 'Image 003b')* supported by fraud 18 below.

Despite IHG Brand Standards demanding that *'Documented evidence of completed training <u>must</u> be maintained'*, and despite a Disclosure Order being in place from Judge Horne for all relevant documents, Employer failed to disclose any training records or certificates to show that Claimant had completed *'advanced'* fire training. These were records that WOULD exist if Claimant had done the *'advanced'* training. Employer managed to disclose a certificate showing that Claimant had done *'advanced'* First Aid training; but Claimant's First Aid training was never in dispute. It's only the training that was in dispute which Employer failed to disclose any records for.

In fraud 2 we demonstrated that Employer falsely stated, or inferred, a *'Supervisor'* and a *'Manager'* were the same roles. That false statement allowed Employer to convince ET that Claimant was a *'Manager'* for over 12 months, rather than just the 3 months he actually was, and therefore he was more likely to have found out specific conditions, procedures and rules relating to being a *'Manager'* during the course of that time. However, whether it was 3 months or over 12 months, the mere fact that Employer relied on Claimant finding out by chance about specific conditions, procedures and rules, demonstrates that Employer themselves knew they had NOT made Claimant aware of them; which is now very relevant to fraud 15 regarding when the Disciplinary Process be initiated.

Image 003a

It was reasonable for the respondent to believe that the claimant, as a highly experienced GSM, knew how to organise a fire evacuation regardless of whether he had attended the same training session as ██ and ██ or indeed any training session under the new management regime.

From Judge Horne's first written refusal to reconsider the Judgment. As you can see, Judge Horne relied on Employer putting forward, or inferring, that Claimant was a 'highly experienced GSM'.

Image 003b

> I therefore find, on the balance of probabilities, that your actions on 2nd January 2015 were a wilful dereliction of a known or appreciated duty on your part which left the hotel at risk.

From Mr Krohn's Disciplinary Appeal Outcome letter. The mere fact that Mr Krohn added 'or appreciated duty' demonstrates he knew or suspected Claimant had NOT been informed of the 'duty' relied on to dismiss him and was covering other options such as Claimant 'finding out by chance' during the course of his employment; otherwise, Mr Krohn would have stopped at 'a known duty' and referenced/disclosed a supporting paper trail of evidence such as training records and certificates.

A later fraud, 18, confirms that Mr Krohn knew that Claimant had not been made aware of relevant information relating to the GSM role.

4. **Employer put to Employment Tribunal, or inferred, that the principal reason for the 2014 Disciplinary Hearing and sanction was the Claimant's Facebook post** – however, undisclosed evidence *(see 'Image 004')* demonstrates that this was a conscious and deliberate dishonesty as the sole reason documented at the time for initiating formal action against Claimant was to send a *'message'* to the *'hotel & the team'*. *'Image 004'* also demonstrates that formal action would be determined prior to any investigation taking place; which in itself made the process unfair as *'Burchell'*, the legal standard for Employment Tribunals, requires that AN INVESTIGATION must be the basis for a belief of guilt. *'Image*

004' further demonstrates that Mr Frodsham *(Disciplinary Officer)* was discussing the issue with Mr Brimacombe *(Investigation Officer)* prior to any investigation taking place, and that Mr Frodsham would decide on formal action without an investigation being conducted or any facts being established; which demonstrates that Mr Frodsham could not be independent when hearing the subsequent Disciplinary.

Image 004

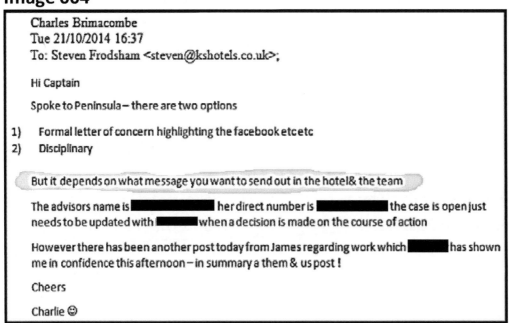

Charles Brimacombe
Tue 21/10/2014 16:37
To: Steven Frodsham <steven@kshotels.co.uk>;

Hi Captain

Spoke to Peninsula – there are two options

1)   Formal letter of concern highlighting the facebook etc etc
2)   Disciplinary

But it depends on what message you want to send out in the hotel & the team

The advisors name is ███████████ her direct number is ███████████ the case is open just needs to be updated with ███████ when a decision is made on the course of action

However there has been another post today from James regarding work which ███████ has shown me in confidence this afternoon – in summary a them & us post !

Cheers

Charlie ☺

Internal email from Mr Brimacombe to Mr Frodsham - prior to any investigation taking place. The action against Claimant would not be dependent on the findings of an 'investigation'; instead, it WOULD be dependent on what 'message' the Employer wanted to send to the 'hotel & the team'.

The 'message' itself is unknown however, the only way to send a 'message' to the 'hotel & the team' would be a public spectacle such as Claimant's Demotion or Dismissal. Any other sanction would be a private matter between Employer and Claimant but, demotion would mean a public change of

job title for Claimant, and dismissal would mean the permanent absence of Claimant from the hotel. The fact that Employer opted for the formal Disciplinary process, before any investigation had taken place, demonstrates that their intention was a public spectacle, be that Claimant's Demotion or Dismissal; this in turn demonstrates pre-determination of guilt and/or outcome.

5. **Peninsula/Employer put to Employment Tribunal, or inferred, that Claimant *'admitted'* to emailing customer personal information to his own private email address** *(see 'Image 005a' and 'Image 005b')*; **Judge Horne took this into account when coming to his decision** *(see 'Image 005c' and 'Image 005d')* – however, this was a conscious and deliberate dishonesty as no such admission was documented in Mr Brimacombe's meeting notes, no such admission was documented in the Disciplinary Notes, no such admission was documented in the Disciplinary Outcome letter, no such admission was documented in the Appeal Notes, and no such admission was documented in the Appeal Outcome letter.

Considering that, at ET, the Employer claimed to have relied on this admission when making their decision to sanction Claimant in 2014, taken with Mr Brimacombe's written statement that the Disciplinary and Appeal Officers *'did not approach me to ask me any questions'* in relation to their respective meetings with Claimant, it is reasonable to conclude that for Employer to have taken such an admission into account, one must have been documented somewhere in the notes of the entire Disciplinary process; yet, the fact that Claimant is NOT documented anywhere as making such an admission demonstrates the likelihood that no such admission was ever made.

Further, no such admission was documented in the Employer's ET3 form to the Employment Tribunal. In fact, the first time Employer alleged Claimant had made such an admission was in their written witness statements to the ET; which demonstrates the allegation was likely fabricated by the Employer solely for the Employment Tribunal.

As *'emailing customer personal information to his own private email address'* was one of two matters which, according to Mr Frodsham at ET, *'amounted to misconduct' (see 'Image 005d')* then, by relying on the issue at ET to justify sanctioning the Claimant without first putting it forward as an allegation or raising it at the Disciplinary Hearing, Claimant was not given a fair opportunity to meet both components of the misconduct argument before being sanctioned.

Image 005a

19. James admitting emailing the photo to his personal email address and admitted that he put the post on Facebook.

From Mr Brimacombe's written statement of 'FACT' to the Employment Tribunal – apparently the Claimant admitted to emailing a photo to his personal email address.

Let's not forget that such an admission would be important information to support Employer's case; yet Mr Brimacombe failed to document any such admission in his handwritten notes, or in his typed up notes, and also failed to pass the information on to the Disciplinary and Appeal Officers.

Image 005b

> a. He admitted emailing a customer's details to a personal email address.
>
> This personal email address isn't owned/monitored/controlled by the hotel or the business. This is therefore 'insecure' in terms of storage our customer's personal information (card details etc.).

From Mr Frodsham's written statement of 'FACT' to the Employment Tribunal – Mr Frodsham states that Claimant admitted 'emailing a customer's details to a personal email address'. However, we know Mr Brimacombe failed to document any such admission in his notes and also failed to pass on any such information to Mr Frodsham, and we know Mr Frodsham failed to document any such admission in the minutes of the Disciplinary Hearing and made no mention of relying on such an admission in the Disciplinary Outcome Letter; therefore, the only place Mr Frodsham could have got that information from was Mr Brimacombe's written statement of 'FACT' to the Employment Tribunal, which Mr Frodsham admitted to reading before he wrote his own statement.

Image 005c

> During Mr Brimacombe's investigation, the claimant stated that he had e-mailed the computer records to his personal e-mail address, used PhotoShop to redact the customer's personal details, and uploaded the altered image to the social media site.

From Judge Horne's written reasons for the Judgment. Judge Horne relied on Mr Brimacombe's written statement regarding Claimant 'emailing' records to himself, despite there being no mention of Claimant doing any such thing in the entire notes from the Disciplinary Process.

26

Image 005d

> What really bothered Mr Frodsham was that it had been inappropriate to put the information on the social media site in the first place. Mr Frodsham was further concerned that the claimant had emailed the unredacted information to his own personal e-mail address. That was an insecure method of handling customer information. In Mr Frodsham's view, these two matters amounted to misconduct. He decided to impose a final written warning.

From Judge Horne's written reasons for the Judgment. Judge Horne relied on Mr Frodsham's written statement regarding Claimant 'emailing' unredacted information to himself; this was again despite there being no mention of Claimant doing any such thing in the entire notes from the Disciplinary Process. Judge Horne also confirms that it was two matters combined which amounted to misconduct.

6. **Peninsula/Employer convinced Judge Horne that Mr Krohn was independent when hearing the Claimant's appeals** *(see 'Image 006a')* – however, undisclosed evidence *(see 'Image 006b')* demonstrates that this was a conscious and deliberate dishonesty as, before any investigation into the 2014 incident had taken place, Mr Krohn had already:-

   I.   discussed the issue with Mr Brimacombe and/or Mr Frodsham,

   II.   discussed the issue with Peninsula,

   III. personally taken charge of the situation by rejecting the informal *'Letter Of Concern' (LOC)* option,

   IV.   already formed an opinion about the Claimant's guilt,

   V.   wanted to deny Claimant his due process by

skipping the disciplinary process and going straight to Gross Misconduct,

VI. and was influential in the action that would be taken against the Claimant *(formal action rather than informal action)*.

This not only went against *'Burchell'*, but also demonstrated that Mr Krohn, who was the last protection of due process within the company, could NOT have been independent when hearing Claimant's Appeals and was unlikely to give Claimant a fair and impartial hearing or correct any mistakes made by Mr Frodsham at Disciplinary stage.

Image 006a

> I accept Mr Crohn's evidence that he kept enough distance away from the actual facts of the case to enable him to be able to hear an appeal independently.

From Judge Horne's written reasons for the Judgment; which speaks for itself.

Image 006b

> Client called up as unhappy with progressing with LOC or disciplinary action wanted to treat as GM. Advised and followed up via email.
>
> Dear Kim,
>
> Further to our call today and I writing to confirm our discussions. I would recommend that Charles holds a investigation meeting with James to discuss the recent incident about the posting on Facebook take minutes of the meeting and forward them onto myself or ▮▮▮▮▮▮.
>
> Following on from the investigation then we can look to take formal disciplinary action so please send over the screen shot and any further evidence that may be of. If Charles discusses any further issues at the meeting then please send me any evidence to support also.
>
> As mentioned I would not advise on suspending James as the allegations do not warrant Gross Misconduct,
>
> 22/10/2014 16:03

Communication between Mr Krohn and Peninsula – prior to

any investigation. In order for Mr Krohn to reject the 'Letter of Concern' (LOC) option, he must first have been informed about it; which demonstrates he discussed the issue with Mr Brimacombe and/or Mr Frodsham.

The fact Mr Krohn then contacted Peninsula directly to reject the LOC and wanted the matter treated as GM (Gross Misconduct) further demonstrates that Mr Krohn was very much involved with the issue early on, had already determined Claimant's guilt, and wanted Claimant dismissed before any investigation had taken place or facts established.

7. **Peninsula/Employer put to Employment Tribunal, or inferred, that the 2014 sanction was decided upon AFTER the disciplinary hearing; therefore it was issued in good faith** – however, undisclosed evidence *(see 'Image 007a' and 'Image 007b')* demonstrates that this was a conscious and deliberate dishonesty as the sanction had been pre-determined 12 days prior to the Disciplinary Hearing taking place; which in itself breached Employment Law.

   A further conscious and deliberate dishonesty was demonstrated on this issue by the fact that Employer, under the approval of Peninsula, removed email evidence from the Tribunal bundle that stated the same as *'Image 007b'*. The removal of the email was only raised with Judge Horne when Claimant requested a reconsideration of the judgment; the email was not allowed as new evidence because it was known about prior to the judgment being made. However, the fact the email was not raised during the Employment Tribunal does NOT negate the fact that the Employer pre-determined the sanction, or that Employer had tampered with evidence by removing the email, or that Peninsula/Employer had falsely convinced Judge Horne that the sanction was issued in good faith.

Image 007a

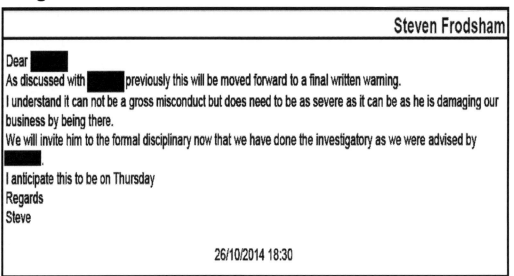

Communication between Employer and Peninsula – prior to Disciplinary Hearing. Even before any 'evidence' has been put to a Disciplinary Hearing, Claimant's guilt and a maximum sanction have already been determined.

Image 007b

Steven Frodsham

Dear ▮

As discussed with ▮ previously this will be moved forward to a final written warning.

I understand it can not be a gross misconduct but does need to be as severe as it can be as he is damaging our business by being there.

We will invite him to the formal disciplinary now that we have done the investigatory as we were advised by ▮.

I anticipate this to be on Thursday

Regards

Steve

26/10/2014 18:30

Communication between Mr Frodsham and Peninsula – prior to Disciplinary Hearing. Mr Frodsham increased the maximum sanction suggested by Peninsula; thereby demonstrating the sanction had been pre-determined twice.

Mr Frodsham also confirmed the issue was NOT one of Gross Misconduct, meaning Claimant can't be dismissed for this offence even if guilt was proven. The maximum sanction allowed by Employer's own procedures in this instance was a 'Written Warning' as suggested by Peninsula; however, Mr Frodsham ignored those procedures and decided that a 'Final Written Warning' will be given in the first instance as the sanction 'needs to be as severe as it can be'.

According to Disciplinary Procedures (see 'Image 010e' of fraud 10), a Final Written Warning may only be issued in the 'first instance' <u>IF</u> Gross Misconduct was alleged <u>AND</u> an investigation showed some level of mitigation for the issue to be treated as an offence just short of dismissal. Mr Frodsham just confirmed the issue wasn't Gross Misconduct and, his 'belief' that Claimant was 'damaging our business' was groundless as it had never been investigated or established by an investigation; therefore issuing a 'Final Written Warning' in this instance breached Employer's own procedures.

The fact Employer couldn't dismiss Claimant in this instance does not negate the fact that we now know Employer's sole intention WAS to dismiss Claimant.

8. **Employer put to Employment Tribunal, or inferred, that a Formal Disciplinary Investigation Meeting was conducted with Claimant before proceeding to the 2014 Disciplinary Hearing** – however, undisclosed evidence *(see 'Image 008a')* demonstrates that this was a conscious and deliberate dishonesty as the meeting Employer cited as an *'Investigation Meeting'* was NOT conducted for reasons of investigation, it was actually an *'Informal 1 to 1 meeting'* reconvened from the previous day and conducted for the sole purpose of bringing Claimant down a peg or two; which

now supports Claimant's statement in the 2014 Disciplinary Notes that he *'was not made aware at any time during his conversation with CB* [Charles Brimacombe] *that it was an investigation meeting'.*

While several issues were discussed at the *'Informal 1 to 1 meeting'*, only the Facebook issue was documented by Mr Brimacombe and those notes were put forward to the ET as *'Formal Investigation Notes'* for the <u>entire</u> meeting.

Further, Mr Brimacombe's undisclosed handwritten notes of the second meeting *(see 'Image 008b' to 'Image 008d')* make no mention of it being an *'investigation meeting'*, that bit was simply added by Mr Brimacombe when he typed up the notes *(see 'Image 008e')*; in essence, Mr Brimacombe falsified the official *'notes'* by giving the impression that only one meeting took place with only one issue being discussed, and further falsified the notes by adding a small statement to the typed up notes which changed the meeting category from an *'informal meeting'* to a *'formal meeting'*.

It has to be noted that an *'Informal Meeting'* was the first step of the Disciplinary Process prior to the franchise agreement coming into force *(see 'Image 008f')*; a step that was still in force up to the end of Sept 2014 and one which allowed for improvement to be shown. Despite Employer not detailing this step in the new Employee Handbook that came into force on 01 Oct 2014, they do make reference to such a step *(see 'Image 008g')* and carried out this step on 24 Oct 2014 with the Claimant; thereby demonstrating it was still part of the Disciplinary Process and that Employer ought to have allowed Claimant time to show improvement before conducting the second meeting or escalating the issue to a

Disciplinary Hearing.

It also has to be noted that nothing documented in the meeting notes could be deemed as *'reasonable grounds'* for the alleged *'beliefs'* that Employer would later rely on at ET to sanction Claimant. Further, Mr Brimacombe did not disclose any *'reasonable grounds'* directly to Mr Frodsham or Mr Krohn at the time, as confirmed in his written statement to Employment Tribunal when he states that both Disciplinary and Appeal Officers *'did not approach me to ask me any questions'*.

Image 008a

To: Steven Frodsham steven@kshotels.co.uk
Sent: 26 Oct 2014, at 00:59,
From: Charles Brimacombe <Charles@hiexpressleigh.co.uk>

Hi

Typed notes from the meeting – informal done yesterday as he was quite strange in attiude & to sound him out as the first thing he said to me when he came in last night is " you want to see me " – so I had him further tonight & documented – not to give him the satisfaction properly last night. I don't know if this has been discussed with anyone else ? But I had a feeling that he new something !

He was more solum tonight - & I think the knowledge that someone has grassed him up has hit home.

However I apologise in advance I did on a separate matter after this – discuss the DM diary situation & how annoyed I am over this – and the childness of it and writing on boards etc – he left pretty deflated – and I think he does not handle confrontation well – its all bravado to collegues at work which is more or less stated in the investigation.

Charlie.

Internal email from Mr Brimacombe, to Mr Frodsham, confirming that a first 'informal' meeting took place on 24 Oct 2014.

Claimant left that meeting with the understanding the issue had been dealt with informally. No time was given for Claimant to show any improvement before a second meeting was held the very next day.

The second meeting ONLY took place because Mr Brimacombe felt Claimant had gained some form of 'satisfaction' from the first meeting.

The second meeting was NOT conducted for the purpose of 'investigation'; nor was it conducted under any provision as set out by the Disciplinary Procedures i.e. there was nothing in those procedures that allowed the Employer to conduct a meeting for the purposes of preventing an employee gaining any 'satisfaction'.

The second meeting was conducted solely to damage Claimant's ego; which it did, as confirmed by Mr Brimacombe when stating 'he was more solum tonight' and left 'deflated'.

Further, note the date and time on the email; Mr Frodsham wrote the Disciplinary Invite letter on 25 Oct 2014 yet, this email was written on 26 Oct 2014, demonstrating that Mr Frodsham wrote the Disciplinary Invite letter BEFORE Mr Brimacombe had reported back to him about the meeting.

Therefore, whether or not this was an 'investigation meeting', it had no relevance to Claimant being invited to a Disciplinary Hearing as Mr Frodsham had already written the invite letter and determined there WAS going to be a hearing.

It has to be noted here that when Mr Brimacombe and Mr Frodsham wrote their statements and gave verbal evidence for the Tribunal, they were fully aware of the 'informal meeting', and the reason for the second meeting, and that the meeting notes were NOT accurate; they knew that NO formal investigation had taken place and knowingly gave false information to the ET.

Image 008b

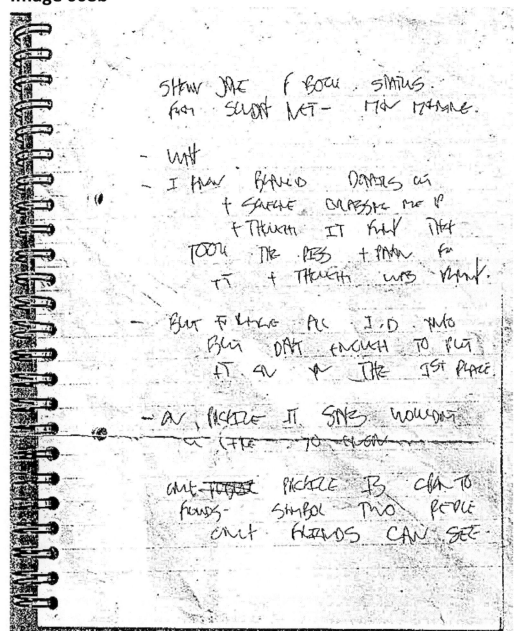

Mr Brimacombe's handwritten meeting notes – page 1

demonstrates that Mr Brimacombe failed to inform Claimant it was an 'investigation meeting' before questioning him.

Image 008c

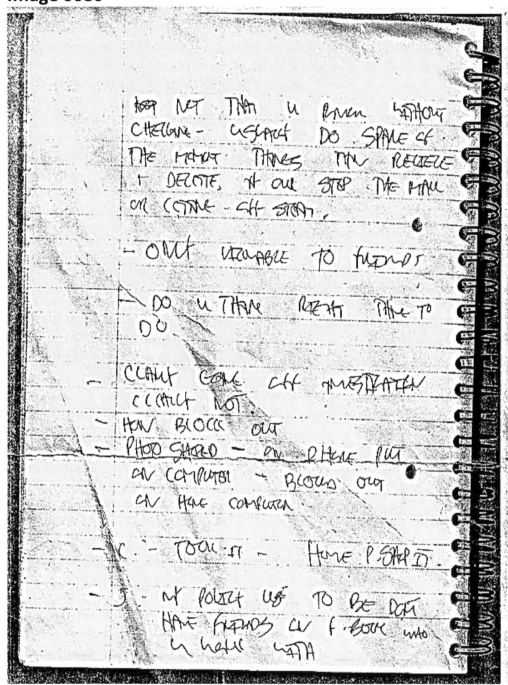

Mr Brimacombe's handwritten meeting notes – page 2; this page and the following page demonstrate that Mr

Brimacombe failed to inform Claimant at any time during the meeting that it was an 'investigation meeting'.

Image 008d

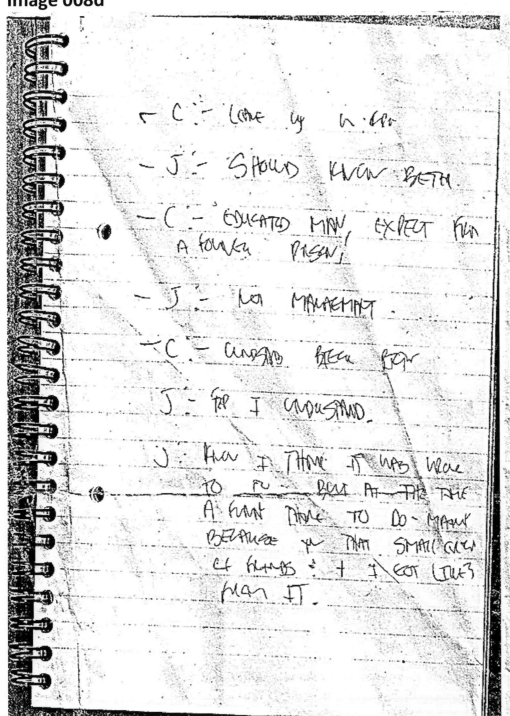

Mr Brimacombe's handwritten meeting notes – page 3. None of the pages were signed and dated by Claimant to confirm this was an accurate account of the meeting.

Image 008e

Investigation Meeting 25th October 2014

James Bagnall

Charles Brimacombe Holding Investigation Meeting

Time Start 22.50pm

Time Finish 23.21

CB :- James I need to ask you some questions concerning Facebook & comments made on it – this is an investigation

JB :- OK

Charles Brimacombe produces the print out of the facebook statement "that was an expensive night's stay . Includes £60.00 I added for cleaning cause he thought it would be fun to throw cereal all over the hotel floors !! " – which James reads

From Mr Brimacombe's typed up meeting notes – with the additional statement 'this is an investigation'. By adding this one small statement Mr Brimacombe is demonstrating that Claimant was NOT informed beforehand that it was an investigation meeting i.e. there would have been no need to inform Claimant at the meeting that it was an investigation if Claimant had already been informed that he was going into an investigation meeting.

The handwritten notes, together with the typed up notes, now demonstrate that Claimant was never informed prior to, or during, the meeting that it was an 'investigation meeting'.

The fact that Mr Brimacombe admits there was an initial 'informal meeting', and that the second meeting was conducted simply for the purpose of preventing Claimant getting 'satisfaction' from the 'informal meeting', demonstrates that NO 'Formal Investigation Meeting' took place before inviting Claimant to a Disciplinary Hearing and issuing him with a 'First & Final Written Warning'; which now amounts to a breach of Employment Law.

Image 008f

> **Disciplinary Action**
> The various stages of disciplinary action are set out below. Disciplinary action will vary depending on the nature of the case. If the misconduct or poor performance is minor or the first occurrence, where appropriate, the line Manager shall discuss the issue on an informal basis with the Team Member as an alternative to invoking the formal disciplinary process. Such discussion should include an explanation by the Manager of the issues and the line Manager should inform the Team Member where remedial action or improvement is required. However, in some cases, such as cases of gross misconduct or other serious misconduct, such preliminary informal discussion will not be appropriate and it may be appropriate for the formal disciplinary procedure to be invoked at one of the stages listed below.
>
> Informal discussion – Note to file
> Stage 1 – Verbal warning
> Stage 2 – 1st written warning
> Stage 3 – Final written warning
> Stage 4 – Dismissal

From the Employee Handbook which was in force prior to 01 Oct 2014. An 'Informal Discussion' is an alternative to invoking the 'Formal Disciplinary Process'.

Although the 24 Oct meeting was not documented, Claimant does recall Mr Brimacombe telling him not to do it again; which would constitute the 'Line Manager' informing the 'Team Member' of the 'remedial action or improvement' required.

Image 008g

> e) other than for an "off the record" informal reprimand, you have the right to be accompanied by a fellow employee at all stages of the formal disciplinary process;

From the Employee Handbook which came into force on 01 Oct 2014. An 'off the record informal reprimand' is confirmed as being an option.

9. **Peninsula/Employer put to Employment Tribunal, or inferred, that Claimant HAD publically posted a *'Customer bill'* onto Facebook in 2014** – however, that was a conscious and deliberate dishonesty as Claimant had demonstrated during the Disciplinary Hearing that the post was NOT of a *'bill'* i.e. it was not a request for payment as it was missing the majority of information required for it to be deemed as a *'bill' (see 'Image 009a' and 'Image 009b')*. No reasonable person would hand over money if presented with a copy of the alleged *'bill'*.

Whatever the post was, it was NOT of a *'bill'*. At ET, the Employer was critical of Claimant for defending against the very specific allegations which they had made against him i.e. that the post was of a *'bill'* and that it contained *'personal information'*. Employer claimed that concentrating on the allegations *'repeatedly distracted away from the general point of concern that Mr Frodsham wanted to discuss'*; Judge Horne relied on this when making his decision *(see 'Image 009c')*.

However, if Employer wanted Claimant to defend against the post being anything other than a *'bill'* containing *'personal information'*, or if they had other issues of concern which they wanted to discuss, they were free to formally state those in the Disciplinary Invite Letter so Claimant could prepare for and defend against them.

In fact, Employer was legally obligated to set out ALL allegations and concerns prior to the Disciplinary Hearing as supported by case law in *'O'Farrill v New Manage Ltd t/a Hooks Gym London Shootfighters'*; that Judgment determined that an employer must set out the nature of the accusations clearly to the employee.

The mere fact that, at ET, the Employer claimed to have issues of concern which they wanted to discuss, but were not disclosed to Claimant prior to the Disciplinary Hearing, demonstrates that they breached Employment Law by not setting out the nature of the accusation clearly to the Claimant; now relevant to fraud 14.

Claimant, on the other hand, was ONLY required to defend against the allegations and concerns that WERE stated in the Disciplinary Invite Letter; which he did when he defended against the post being of a *'bill'* containing *'personal information'*. Each time Employer hijacked the meeting, by introducing new allegations and concerns that had not been formally put in the Disciplinary Invite Letter, Claimant was forced to repeatedly bring the conversation back to the officially stated allegations and concerns.

As for the post being open to the public; Claimant had already referred to a symbol on the post that signifies it was only viewable by those in Claimant's extremely small Facebook group. The fact that Employer couldn't view the post directly and had to instruct Miss Snitch to take a screenshot of it *(see 'Image 009d')*, thereby circumventing Claimant's Facebook security measures, demonstrates that the post was NOT open to the public, that it was unlikely to be seen by the unidentified subject of the post or their company, and that Employer had to use underhanded measures to obtain evidence.

Image 009a

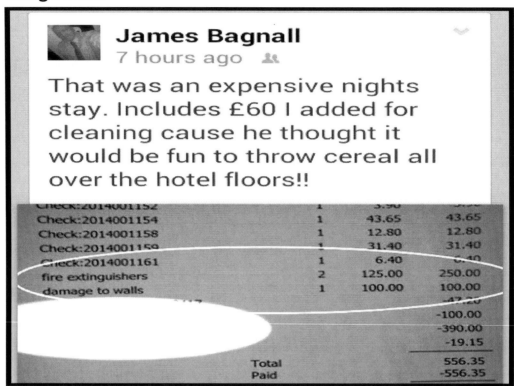

Check:2014001152	1	3.90	
Check:2014001154	1	43.65	43.65
Check:2014001158	1	12.80	12.80
Check:2014001159	1	31.40	31.40
Check:2014001161	1	6.40	6.40
fire extinguishers	2	125.00	250.00
damage to walls	1	100.00	100.00
			-100.00
			-390.00
			-19.15
Total			556.35
Paid			-556.35

This is the entire post on Facebook, which was private to a handful of Claimant's friends; therefore no genuine risk to the Employer's reputation.

It was not altered after the screenshot was taken; this is it, as it could be viewed directly by Claimant's friends, and as the screenshot was viewed by Employer. Nothing in the post identifies the person concerned, or the company they worked for, or the hotel, or the franchise which the hotel traded as.

In fact, nothing in Claimant's entire Facebook page identified his employer. Again, there was no genuine risk to the Employer's reputation.

Note the symbol next to '7 hours ago'; that signifies the post was only directly viewable by those in Claimant's group. Had the post been open 'for all to see', as Employer maintained it was, that symbol would have been a globe.

The Employer subsequently disclosed this screenshot in the Employment Tribunal bundle, which went on public display for two days; much longer than it was displayed on Facebook and to a much wider audience than Facebook because everyone, including members of the public attending the Tribunal, had full access to the screenshot. Peninsula also handed a spare copy of the bundle to one member of the public on request after the Employment Tribunal had ended; we have no idea how many other people have seen the screenshot from that bundle or if further copies were made and distributed.

Therefore, it was Peninsula/Employer who made the screenshot publicly available and, in doing so, demonstrated that they saw no detrimental effect to Employer's business by it being made public.

Image 009b

Parliament / The Government are the highest authority in the land. They set the laws and standards for this country. Of the many standards they have set, one of them is the attributes that <u>MUST</u> be included on a bill / invoice.

Those attributes are as follows:-

1) **must clearly display the word 'invoice' on the document.**
2) **must include a unique identification number**
3) **must include your company name, address and contact information**
4) **must include the company name and address of the customer you're invoicing**
5) must include a clear description of what you're charging for
6) **must include the date the goods or service were provided (supply date)**
7) **must include the date of the invoice**
8) must include the amount(s) being charged
9) **must include VAT amount if applicable**
10) must include the total amount owed

Of the 10 attributes that <u>MUST</u> be included on a bill, 7 are not present. Therefore, according to The Government, who are the highest authority in the land, this screenshot is not of a bill. This, in turn, means no customer bill was distributed onto social media. As a result, this stated matter of concern is disproved.

From Claimant's notes that he read out at the 2014 Disciplinary Hearing.

Image 009c

> 24. The claimant was then invited to a disciplinary meeting, chaired by Mr Frodsham. The invitation letter set out an allegation that the claimant had published personal information in a customer's bill on social media.
>
> 25. Sadly, the meeting was rather dysfunctional. The claimant concentrated on technical definitions in the allegations in the invitation letter such as the legal definition of a "bill" and the definition of "personal information" in the Data Protection Act 1998. As a result, the conversation was repeatedly distracted away from the general point of concern that Mr Frodsham wanted to discuss.

From Judge Horne's written reasons for the Judgment. The allegation against Claimant was that he posted a 'bill' on social media which contained 'personal information'; a very specific and serious allegation. Claimant demonstrated that the post was NOT of a 'bill' and that the post DID NOT contain 'personal information'.

What Judge Horne deemed as 'claimant concentrated on technical definitions', was Claimant defending against the very specific allegations made against him. What Judge Horne deemed as 'the conversation was repeatedly distracted away from the general point of concern', was Claimant repeatedly bringing the conversation back to the officially stated points of concern each time Mr Frodsham hijacked the Disciplinary Hearing by introducing new points of concerns and allegations that were not stated in the Disciplinary Invite Letter.

Employer, with 'expert' advice from Peninsula, chose the allegations and concerns which they wanted to put to Claimant at the Disciplinary Hearing; if there was a 'general point of concern that Mr Frodsham wanted to discuss', Employer had every opportunity to include it in the Disciplinary Invite Letter so Claimant could prepare for and address it. What Employer can't do is hijack a Disciplinary

Hearing by introducing new allegations and concerns part way through without any formal notice.

Image 009d

> 24. ███████, who is a guest services manager, came to me and told me that she had seen something on Facebook from James' profile. I asked her to take a picture of it and send it to me. She did (see **page 227**) and I passed it to Charlie to investigate.

From Mr Frodsham's written statement to the Employment Tribunal. Claimant had implemented security measures on his Facebook page to prevent those not in his group from seeing his posts. Mr Frodsham couldn't take a screenshot of the post, and neither could Mr Brimacombe, because they were NOT in Claimant's Facebook group; Mr Frodsham therefore requested that Miss Snitch take the screenshot as she was in Claimant's Facebook group; in essence, Mr Frodsham circumvented Claimant's Facebook security in order to obtain evidence to use against him.

10. **Peninsula/Employer put to Employment Tribunal, or inferred, that Claimant's Facebook post contained *'Customer Personal Information'* which damaged the business** *(see 'Image 010a')* – however, undisclosed evidence *(see 'Image 010b' to 'Image 010d')* demonstrates that this was a conscious and deliberate dishonesty as Peninsula had already informed Employer several times during the disciplinary process that the Claimant's post DID NOT contain any such personal information therefore *'no loss'* to the business.

Further, no investigation was carried out to determine what, if any, damage was caused to the business or how such damage would be measured; which demonstrates that Employer could not have had a genuine belief, as required by *'Burchell'*, that the Claimant was guilty of damaging the business. Disciplinary Procedures themselves demanded that an investigation MUST show actual damage in order to issue a *'First & Final Written Warning' (see 'Image 010e')*; *'potential for damage'* would not meet those requirements.

Disciplinary Procedures are there to be followed. If Employer doesn't like the procedures which THEY put in place, they can change them; what they can't do is violate them to issue a sanction.

Image 010a

On 13th November 2014 the Claimant was given a first and final written warning for an action of serious misconduct as the result of a disciplinary hearing conducted under the Respondent's disciplinary procedure. Namely, publicly distributing customer information on social media bringing the company into disrepute and breaching trust. The Claimant was informed of his right of appeal in the decision letter.

Taken from Employer's ET3 form to Employment Tribunal. Despite Peninsula/Employer confirming with each other at least three times prior to issuing the 2014 sanction that NO customer information was published by Claimant (as demonstrated in 'Image 010b' to 'Image 010d'), Peninsula/Employer still put to ET that Claimant published customer information.

Image 010b

Client believes his original action of posting pictures on Facebook is GM (client has sought advice from solicitor who also believes this is GM) - client sent across screen shots while on the call - advised that these do not show any personal details looking at it now I would not be able to see what it is about and no loss gained therefore difficult to constitute GM.

Client to send reschedule letter across to me for review.
30/10/2014 14:49

Communication between Employer and Peninsula – prior to Disciplinary Hearing and confirming there is NO personal information in the picture.

Image 010c

Advised client no personal information placed on the picture I would not be able to establish who it was - First & Final Written Warning is at a push and I will draft the outcome as need to make it as strong as possible to strongly justify how severe you have taken it, may need to review actions in future as may not be strong enough to build on dismissal - I will draft the letter and send full details of case and future steps so you and Kim are clear on progress.
11/11/2014 14:27

Communication between Employer and Peninsula – prior to Disciplinary Outcome letter being written and again confirming there is NO personal information in the picture.

Image 010d

HI Steven,

apologies in the delay in getting this across to you, please read the attached and confirm it is a true reflection of hat was discussed, if you wish to add anything further to the letter of why you believe his behaviour was unacceptable then please do as you need to make this strong as possible.

As per our telephone call and as previous calls with Kim the fact that no personal information was on the post weakens the case significantly and this First & Final Written Warning is being issued at a push. As discussed if he commits further acts of conduct they would have to be strong in order for you to build on this warning to progress to dismissal stages.

If you do make any changes to the letter then please send back for final approval before issuing.
12/11/2014 11:42

Communication between Mr Frodsham and Peninsula – prior to Disciplinary Outcome letter being written and once again confirming there is NO personal information in the picture.

Image 010e

D) SERIOUS MISCONDUCT

1) Where one of the unsatisfactory conduct or misconduct rules has been broken and if, upon investigation, it is shown to be due to your extreme carelessness or has a serious or substantial effect upon our operation or reputation, you may be issued with a final written warning in the first instance.

2) You may receive a final written warning as the first course of action, if, in an alleged gross misconduct disciplinary matter, upon investigation, there is shown to be some level of mitigation resulting in it being treated as an offence just short of dismissal.

From Employee Handbook (which formed part of Claimant's contract of employment).

Item '1' clearly states that IF an investigation shows a 'serious or substantial effect', only then may a 'Final Written Warning' be issued in the first instance.

Item '2' is relevant to 'Image 007b' of fraud 7.

11. **Employer put to Employment Tribunal, or inferred, that disclosure of 'Personal information' was a genuine concern of theirs, hence the 2014 Disciplinary** – however, as demonstrated by Employer's own actions, that was a conscious and deliberate dishonesty as they held themselves to a lower standard than Claimant and had no problem in disclosing employee/customer/others *'Personal Information'* when it suited them for example:-

    I.   Employer conducted Claimant's Workplace Stress Assessment, and discussed his health condition, in an open bar with guest around instead of in a private room. No concern from Employer that people in the bar might hear Claimant's *'personal information'*.

48

II.   Employer conducted Claimant's 2015 Disciplinary Investigation in an open bar with guests around instead of in a private room; a meeting that is twice documented as being interrupted by guests. Again, no concern from Employer that people in the bar might hear Claimant's *'personal information'*.

III.   Employer verbally disclosed, to an Employment Tribunal courtroom filled with members of the public, that the hotel Chef had a drinking problem. That was *'personal information'* belonging to the Chef which had not previously been disclosed; Employer made that medical information public without any concern for their obligations under the Data Protection Act.

IV.   Employer disclosed *'personal information'* online belonging to a reviewer who had left a scathing review for the hotel *(see 'Image 011a')*. Employer had no concerns in disclosing *'personal information'* when they wanted to score points against someone.

V.   More recently, the Employer posted footage from the hotel CCTV system onto Facebook in an effort to identify a group of kids *(see 'Image 011b')*; because the kids were identifiable in the footage it became their *'personal information'*. Posting the footage on Facebook was a breach of Data Protection as Employer was not registered to collect and process CCTV data for that purpose. The Employer had no concern for the disclosure of *'personal information'* belonging to those kids, nor did they have any concern about repercussions on the wellbeing/safety of those kids as a result of posting the footage which had been viewed 38.6 thousand times with several comments advocating violence or harm towards the kids *(see 'Image 011c' and 'Image 011d')*.

Disclosure of *'Personal information'* was NOT a genuine concern for the Employer; any concern held by Employer about *'Personal information'* relating to Claimant's actions was superficial in order to use the *'Personal information'* argument as a tool to sanction Claimant.

Image 011a

Employer's public online response to a scathing review of their hotel, which is still online and has been for over 5 years

(their response was lengthy so we have edited it down to the relevant points) – Employer discloses that the reviewer tried to cheat the online booking system by attempting to use a discounted 'corporate rate' for a day on which they were not allowed to use that rate. Then Employer discloses contents of a private note regarding the reviewer. Then Employer discloses the price that reviewer's room was reduced to. Then Employer discloses the final total reviewer was charged for their room i.e. the entire room charge was refunded.

Considering that Claimant was sanctioned for privately disclosing similar information about an unidentifiable person, we find it hypocritical that Employer would then publicly disclose such information regarding an identifiable person; a clear case of Employer holding Claimant to a higher standard than they held for themselves.

Image 011b

Holiday Inn Express Leigh - Sports Village

14 July ·

Literally every day we are getting damage from kids passing the hotel to get to Pennington Flash. This was today's instalment at 12.33. The police told us yesterday there is not much they can do, despite us passing on the name of the person who did it last time. They are too busy with other crimes, and he's only 14!! Absolutely shameful. #Leigh #leighsportsvillage

57   53 comments 338 shares

Screenshot from Employer's Facebook page showing video

footage they posted from the hotel's CCTV system on 14 July 2020 (the faces were not covered on the video when it was posted on Facebook, we have covered the faces on the screenshot for this publication) – it was shared 338 times just from this page alone, but no way of knowing how many times the footage was subsequently shared from those users.

After a complaint to the ICO in Sept 2020, the Employer was forced to remove the CCTV footage as it breached Data Protection (or GDPR as it is now known as).

This demonstrates double standards when it comes to disclosing personal information; Employer sanctioned Claimant for 'allegedly' posting 'Personal Information' onto Facebook, and here we have the Employer themselves actually posting 'Personal Information' onto Facebook.

Image 011c

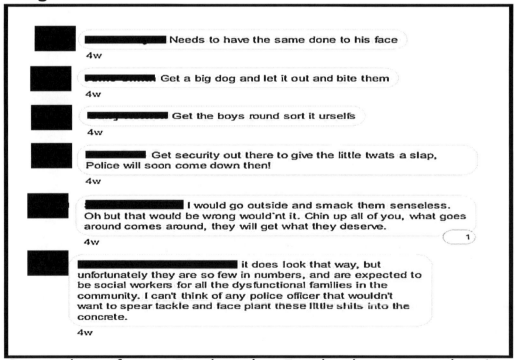

Screenshot from Employer's Facebook page showing

comments encouraging violence or harm toward the kids in the CCTV footage; a direct response to the CCTV footage being published (we have blocked out the user names and pictures for this publication). The fact Employer left these comments online for 4 weeks, and only removed them when forced to do so by the ICO, demonstrates that Employer themselves had little regard for the consequences of 'Personal Information' being published when Claimant was not involved in making the post.

Image 011d

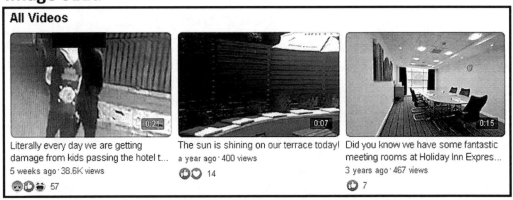

Screenshot from Employer's Facebook page showing a list of videos they had uploaded. In just 5 weeks the video containing the 'Personal Information' of children had greatly outperformed the other two videos put together and been viewed 38.6 thousand times; yet Claimant's post was viewed a handful of times, didn't contain 'Personal Information', didn't have comments encouraging violence or harm towards children, and he was issued with a sanction just short of dismissal.

12. **Peninsula/Employer put to Employment Tribunal, or inferred, that the 2014 sanction was issued as per Employer disciplinary procedures** – however, as demonstrated in fraud 7, that was a conscious and deliberate dishonesty as the

2014 sanction was pre-determined.

Had the sanction not been pre-determined it would still not meet the requirements set out by the Disciplinary Procedures as demonstrated in *'Image 007b'* of fraud 7 i.e. the offence was NOT Gross Misconduct, and as demonstrated in *'Image 010e'* of fraud 10 i.e. *'serious or substantial effect'* was NOT established by an investigation. It is further demonstrated in the *'Meeting Notes'* that NONE of the alleged facts Employer relied on were investigated, let alone *'carefully investigated'* as required by the Disciplinary Procedures *(see 'Image 012')*. Again, Disciplinary Procedures are there to be followed. If Employer doesn't like the procedures which THEY put in place, they can change them; what they can't do is violate them to issue a sanction.

Image 012

d) you will only be disciplined after careful investigation of the facts and the opportunity to present your side of the case. On some occasions temporary suspension on contractual pay may be necessary in order that an uninterrupted investigation can take place. This must not be regarded as disciplinary action or a penalty of any kind;

e) other than for an "off the record" informal reprimand, you have the right to be accompanied by a fellow employee at all stages of the formal disciplinary process;

From Employee Handbook; 'Careful investigation of the facts' implies a much higher standard of investigation than would normally be conducted. However, in both the 2014 and 2015 Disciplinary Processes, the notes disclosed to ET demonstrate that the alleged facts relied on by Employer were NOT investigated at all, let alone carefully investigated; the alleged facts relied on were simply bias personal opinions from the Employer with no supporting evidence from an investigation.

While the act of conducting 'an' investigation met the bare minimum required by THIS Employment Tribunal (despite

Employer not investigating or establishing the actual facts they relied on), failing to carefully investigate the facts breached the Disciplinary Procedures put in place by the Employer, which in turn breached the Claimant's Employment Contract as those procedures formed part of that contract.

13. **Peninsula/Employer put to Employment Tribunal, or inferred, that the 2015 dismissal was decided upon AFTER the disciplinary hearing; therefore it too was in good faith** – however, undisclosed evidence *(see 'Image 013a and 'Image 013b")* demonstrates that this was a conscious and deliberate dishonesty as that sanction was also pre-determined and therefore the dismissal was in bad faith and breached Employment Law.

Image 013a

Client called - confirmed key question is why he chose not to call when he knew colleague wasn't coming in sick.

Meeting due 9am

Client looking for pre-drafted letter to confirm dismissal. Advised will start putting one together but shouldn't make it look like decision was pre-conceived. Advised can telephone the outcome following the meeting with dismissal letter to follow afterwards.

28/01/2015 19:44

Communication between Employer and Peninsula – a day prior to the reconvened Disciplinary Hearing taking place. The fact that a 'pre-drafted letter to confirm dismissal' was requested by Employer demonstrates they had already determined the outcome would be dismissal. The fact that Peninsula warns about making the decision look pre-conceived demonstrates they know/suspect it is pre-conceived. The fact that the dismissal letter WAS going to follow the 'outcome phone call' further demonstrates that Employer HAS already determined the outcome will be dismissal.

Image 013b

> Notice period as per contract - started May 2009 so five weeks.
>
> Discussed what happens if employee doesn't answer his phone. Advised
>
> ---
>
> First draft attached - have a read over please, needs some additions and dates included but please feel free to add anything extra or remove anything you feel isn't relevant. I'll be back in tomorrow morning to discuss further.
> 28/01/2015 21:32

Communication between Employer and Peninsula – a day prior to the reconvened Disciplinary Hearing taking place. The fact that Claimant's notice period is discussed demonstrates a dismissal is being considered. The fact that Peninsula advised on what to do if Claimant doesn't answer his phone to receive the outcome demonstrates an 'immediate' dismissal without notice has been determined because, Claimant not answering his phone wouldn't be an issue unless the sanction required him not to attend work on the night the outcome was disclosed to him. The fact that the first draft of the 'pre-drafted letter to confirm dismissal' is attached further demonstrates the sanction HAS already been determined.

14. **Peninsula/Employer put to Employment Tribunal, or inferred, that the 2015 Disciplinary Process was conducted fairly** – however, undisclosed evidence *(see 'Image 014a' to 'Image 014f')* demonstrates that this was a conscious and deliberate dishonesty as, rather than seeking balanced evidence from both sides in order to make a fair decision, Employer was directed by Peninsula to look solely for evidence against Claimant.

Even then, after reviewing everything available, Peninsula concluded that a dismissal would NOT be fair in this instance and stated they would NOT endorse a dismissal; nothing damaging to Claimant was established after that to cause

Peninsula's view to change but, evidence was found which supported Claimant and cast doubt on what he knew at the time in relation to Managers being on site. That evidence *(see 'Image 014g')* was subsequently withheld.

There were also breaches to Employment Law, as detailed in frauds 9, 16 and 17; which, by definition, demonstrate that a fair Disciplinary Process was not conducted.

Image 014a

> ████████████
>
> No procedure in place - a focus of the meeting would be drill down onto times where he has followed the correct procedure.
>
> Just in case we do not give a dismissal, good idea we can conceal the names on witness statements.
>
> 13/01/2015 12:50

Communication between Employer and Peninsula – prior to the Disciplinary Hearing. Peninsula confirmed that there were NO procedures in place; therefore Claimant hasn't breached any procedures. Peninsula ought to advise Employer at this point to go back and determine what the issue was and what rule was broken; in fact, that should have been done prior to sending out the Disciplinary Invite Letter.

Instead, Peninsula advised Employer to go ahead with the Disciplinary Hearing and to concentrate on something else entirely i.e. 'drill down onto times when he has followed the correct procedures'. Following correct procedures, and not having procedures in place to follow, are two different things; the first is the responsibility of ALL staff, the latter is solely the responsibility of the Employer. Claimant shouldn't be held responsible for Employer's failure to have procedures in place.

You will also notice that, even at this early stage, Dismissal seems to be a foregone conclusion as demonstrated when

Peninsula advise the Employer on a precaution to take 'just in case' Claimant isn't dismissed.

Image 014b

> ▉▉▉▉▉▉▉▉
>
> No issue with you taking disciplinary.. the facts are not in dispute. The disciplinary is to hear mitigation.
>
> 20/01/2015 12:50

Communication between Employer and Peninsula – prior to the Disciplinary Hearing. According to Peninsula 'the facts are not in dispute'; however, none of the 'facts' Employer will rely on to dismiss Claimant have been 'carefully' investigated, established, or put to Claimant yet, so of course they are not in dispute.

On the back of 'undisputed facts' that were NOT established and NOT disclosed to Claimant, Peninsula advise that the Disciplinary Hearing is simply 'to hear mitigation'; thereby demonstrating that Claimant's guilt has already been determined and that the hearing is 'just in case' Claimant can put forward anything to change their minds.

Image 014c

> ▉▉▉▉▉▉▉
>
> Would have recomended an extension of the final written warning anyway.
> Do not think it will be safe dismissal but will review the documents he has submitted anyway and get back to you before 12pm tomorrow.
>
> 21/01/2015 16:47

Communication between Employer and Peninsula – after the Disciplinary Hearing has been adjourned. Peninsula are of the opinion that a dismissal will NOT be safe; thereby demonstrating that a dismissal is being considered by Employer before the Disciplinary Process has been completed.

Image 014d

> Steven Frodsham
>
> Nothing in writing from the hotel. Then again you cannot list everything in handbook.
>
> 22/01/2015 13:36

Communication between Employer and Peninsula – a day after the Disciplinary Hearing has been adjourned. Employer confirms that there is 'nothing in writing from the hotel'. This demonstrates that Claimant hasn't breached any conditions, rules or procedures in the handbook or written elsewhere; which supported the Claimant's argument but was not disclosed to him or to the Employment Tribunal.

Image 014e

> ███████████
>
> Fine to to reconvene hearing but with the additional witness statements. This is only if we can show this - he made a judgement call, and got it wrong.
>
> On that I would say it was unsatisfactory conduct and recommend that FFW is extended. Smacks of an unfair dismissal claim.
>
> Dismissal is not going to be something I would endorse.
>
> 22/01/2015 13:36

Communication between Employer and Peninsula – a day after the Disciplinary Hearing has been adjourned. Having read all the meeting documents, which Employer conveniently failed to include in the Tribunal bundle, Peninsula are now of the opinion that Claimant 'made a judgement call, and got it wrong'.

Peninsula determined that a dismissal in this instance would be unfair and stated they would NOT endorse such a dismissal. This demonstrates that, at this point 22 Jan 2015, employer had no reasonable grounds to dismiss Claimant fairly; which they failed to disclose to Employment Tribunal.

Image 014f

> Advised client the lack of a written procedure regarding handovers is problematic. Nothing in handbook to hang this on.
>
> Advised that if we could evidence he's acted differently in the past then we might be onto something. Employee is saying he thinks he's done nothing wrong. If we can show he's always made the phonecall in the past then we might have something. Client to look into this and agreed to speak again at 730pm.
>
> 22/01/2015 19:10

Communication between Employer and Peninsula – a day after the Disciplinary Hearing has been adjourned. Peninsula again confirmed there were no written procedures and 'Nothing in handbook to hang this on'. This once again demonstrates that Claimant hasn't breached any conditions, rules or procedures in the handbook, or written elsewhere (as established in previous 'Image 014d'); thereby supporting that, at this point 22 Jan 2015, employer had no reasonable grounds to initiate the formal Disciplinary Process let alone carry on with it and dismiss Claimant.

A reasonable employer might now conclude that this probably wasn't a misconduct issue because no specific conditions, rules or procedures were breached; they may even update their procedures so issues like this do not happen again. Employer themselves could well have come to that conclusion had Peninsula not directed them to go and find something to 'hang this on'.

Image 014g

> Client thinks there may be a training course that this employee was involved in that emphasises the need for a senior person on site. Client getting that now and calling me back.
>
> 22/01/2015 19:51

> There is a document that says need GSM between 7-11, however JB won't have seen this.
>
> 22/01/2015 20:50

Communication between Employer and Peninsula – a day after the Disciplinary Hearing has been adjourned. Employer only 'thinks' Claimant may have done certain training regarding Management being on site.

After an hour of searching for information on just one issue to use against Claimant (an amount of time that greatly exceeded the 10 minutes Employer gave to Claimant's entire investigation meeting), Employer can only confirm that there is a document regarding the issue but Claimant wouldn't have seen it. This information was relevant evidence to support that Claimant would NOT have known a manager had to be on site at ALL times, but Employer never disclosed it to Claimant during the Disciplinary Hearing or to the Employment Tribunal.

15. **Peninsula/Employer put to Employment Tribunal, or inferred, that the 2015 sanction was issued as per Employer disciplinary procedures** – however, as demonstrated in fraud 13, that was a conscious and deliberate dishonesty as the 2015 sanction was pre-determined.

    Had the sanction not been pre-determined it would still not meet the requirements set out by the Disciplinary Procedures *(see previous 'Image 012')* as demonstrated by the Investigation Notes; NONE of the alleged facts Employer relied on were investigated let alone *'carefully investigated'* as required by those procedures.

    Once again, Disciplinary Procedures are there to be followed. If Employer doesn't like the procedures which THEY put in place, they can change them; what they can't do is violate them to issue a sanction.

Also, Employer completely ignored the fact that their own Staff Handbook, which came into force on 01 Oct 2014, clearly stated *'Staff must not stay on the premises once they have finished work'*; a condition/rule that had no exceptions concerning lack of Managers.

Therefore, when Claimant left the hotel that morning he was complying with the Staff Handbook. Employer could have used this issue as a learning curve to revise their rules and procedures by adding an exception, but they didn't.

Further, Employer had the option to use a lesser sanction on the Claimant i.e. demotion, but instead relied on criteria not provided for in the Disciplinary Procedures to circumvent that option *(see 'Image 015a')*.

The new evidence, which Peninsula/Employer failed to disclose, also demonstrates an argument that the Disciplinary Procedures themselves should not have been used in this instance *(see 'Image 015b')* as the disciplinary issue was not a specific example shown in the handbook or written elsewhere, as confirmed previously by Peninsula/Employer when they stated *'nothing in handbook to hang this on'* and *'nothing in writing from the hotel'*.

The issue was also not regarding a specific condition, procedure or rule made known to the Claimant, as confirmed by Employer when they informed Peninsula *'there is a document'* but *'Claimant would not have seen it'* (detailed in *fraud 18)* a fact which Claimant indicated during the Appeal process *(see 'Image 015c')*, and which was supported by the fact that Employer's defence relied solely on Claimant finding out by chance what the specific conditions, procedures or rules were due to his length of service as a Manager rather than Employer themselves making those things known to him.

Image 015a

Hello Kim

Thanks for your emails. I don't perceive any real substantial difference, so I advise that we agree to what he states. I'm proposing we don't comment on his query about the line "...conduct during this process". For your own information - that line refers to the fact he demonstrated no remorse or acknowledgment of the concerns caused by his leaving the hotel without appropriate managerial authority and failing to let anybody know. Contrition can be a mitigating factor - had he said sorry, he knew and accepts he should have done differently - then we could well have decided upon a lesser sanction because there would have been the possibility that this remained someone we could work with.

26/02/2015 19:56

Communication between Employer and Peninsula – during the adjournment. Peninsula confirms that Claimant could have received a lesser sanction had he said 'sorry' and 'accepts he should have done differently' then 'there would have been the possibility that this remained someone we could work with'.

The Disciplinary Procedures had a provision which allowed for a lesser sanction to be considered IF the Employee was a Manager and the offence was NOT one of Gross Misconduct. In this instance, the Claimant was a Manager and the offence was NOT Gross Misconduct; therefore 'demotion' was an option for Employer to consider. Nowhere in those procedures is there a requirement that, before 'demotion' can be considered, an employee must say 'sorry'.

Claimant stated at both Disciplinary and Appeal Hearings that he would, in future, phone Mr Frodsham rather than just email him; therefore demonstrating that Claimant had learned from his mistake and would do things differently.

From 02 Jan onwards, and throughout the Disciplinary Process, the Employer continued to leave Claimant alone and in charge of the hotel; therefore demonstrating that Employer had no genuine concerns in working with Claimant despite his actions on 02 Jan 2015.

Further, the fact that Claimant had complied with all the required conduct improvements from the 2014 Disciplinary is evidence that he could follow instructions WHEN they were given to him. That now left saying 'sorry' as the only obstacle in the way of Employer considering a 'demotion'; which demonstrates that the Employer applied criteria, in order to dismiss Claimant, which was not provided for in the Disciplinary Procedures.

Peninsula/Employer are both aware that a lesser sanction could have been used at the Disciplinary Hearing; one which was still available for them to use at Appeal Hearing in order to overturn the dismissal. However, Employer failed to consider a lesser sanction because they applied the non-existent criteria of 'saying sorry'.

Image 015b

> B) DISCIPLINARY RULES
>
> It is not practicable to specify all disciplinary rules or offences that may result in disciplinary action, as they may vary depending on the nature of the work. In addition to the specific examples of unsatisfactory conduct, misconduct and gross misconduct shown in this handbook, a breach of other specific conditions, procedures, rules etc. that are contained within this handbook or that have otherwise been made known to you, will also result in this procedure being used to deal with such matters.

Before initiating Disciplinary Procedures the Employer was obligated to establish that Claimant had breached a specific condition, procedure or rule contained within the handbook or one that HAD 'been made known' to him.

Regarding the 2014 Disciplinary; in that instance the Employer could point to a specific condition in the handbook to support using the Disciplinary Procedures. Yet, despite that, the Employer still failed to 'carefully investigate' and establish any of the facts they relied on; instead, the Employer pre-determined the sanction.

Regarding the 2015 Disciplinary; in that instance Peninsula/Employer established that there was 'nothing in the handbook to hang this on' and 'nothing written from the hotel'. As there was nothing written to rely on, Employer now had to establish that any specific conditions, procedures or rules HAD 'been made known' to Claimant.

Employer had already established that Claimant would not have seen a relevant document regarding Managers being on site, and subsequently failed to give any instance of when specific conditions, procedures or rules WERE 'made known' to Claimant. Instead, Employer relied solely on Claimant's exaggerated length of service as a Manager as grounds that he 'ought to have known' those things; however, the provision in the Disciplinary Procedures was very clear in that specific conditions, procedures or rules MUST be 'made known' to an employee, which did not allow for an employee 'finding out by chance'.

The mere fact that Employer's argument relied solely on Claimant finding out by chance, during the course of his Manager role, as to what the specific conditions procedures or rules were, demonstrates that Employer themselves knew they had NOT made those things 'known' to Claimant.

Employer letting Claimant 'find out by chance' is also

confirmed in the 'Workplace Stress Assessment' conducted on 01 Jan 2015, and in Claimant's Disciplinary Appeal Letter (see 'Image 015c'), when Claimant states that there is no communication from Employer 'unless you do something wrong' i.e. you only find out what the rules are when you break them.

Image 015c

The first time there was ever any indication that management should be on site, before I go home, was at the investigation meeting prior to this disciplinary. That is over six months after this company had taken over. This is typical mode of operation for this company, they don't communicate much until you do something wrong

From Claimant's 2015 Appeal letter to Mr Krohn. Claimant had told Employer several times during the Disciplinary Hearing that 'there are no procedures that I have been made aware of' and 'if there are such procedures then I have never been informed about these'. Claimant then told Mr Krohn at Appeal stage that in the six months they had owned the hotel they had not once informed him of any such procedures and that he only found out what they were by unintentionally breaking them.

The onus was on Employer to establish that any specific conditions, procedures or rules HAD 'been made known' to Claimant; Employer failed to establish any such thing therefore Employer breached their own Disciplinary Procedures by continuing to use those procedures in this instance. And we now know that Mr Krohn and Peninsula KNEW before Claimant's dismissal, let alone at the Appeal Hearing, that Claimant had not seen a relevant document regarding Management being on site.

16. **Peninsula/Employer put to Employment Tribunal, or inferred, that on the morning of 24 Oct 2014 Claimant stayed over at work to cover for a Manager absence** (see 'Image 016a' to 'Image 016f'); **thereby establishing that Claimant knew what to do on 02 Jan 2015 when another Manager was absent for their shift** – however, undisclosed evidence (see 'Image 016g' to 'Image 016j') demonstrates that this was a conscious and deliberate dishonesty as, during the Claimant's Appeal process, Peninsula/Employer established that Claimant wasn't in work on the morning of 24 Oct 2014; Peninsula even questioned Employer as to why they were relying on the incident if it didn't happen.

Further, as confirmed by the notes of the entire Disciplinary Process, and subsequently confirmed by Judge Horne in his first written refusal to reconsider the judgment (see 'Image 016k'), this alleged incident was NOT put to Claimant during the Disciplinary Hearing; it was simply relied on to dismiss him afterwards without it being investigated.

Not only did that breach Employer's own Disciplinary Procedures, which in turn breached Claimant's contract of employment, it also breached Employment Law i.e. *'O'Farrill v New Manage Ltd t/a Hooks Gym London Shootfighters'*; in that Judgment it was stated that ANY disciplinary sanction MUST be imposed ONLY in respect of allegations that WERE properly investigated AND brought to the employee's attention as part of the proceedings. This is now relevant to previous fraud 14.

Image 016a

> 49.   Mr Frodsham considered that, when there was a shortage of cover, the claimant knew that he had to telephone a manager to arrange a replacement and to stay on the premises until the replacement had arrived. Evidence of such knowledge was, in Mr Frodsham's opinion, to be found in the way the claimant had acted in the past. Mr Frodsham put this point to the claimant in general terms at the disciplinary meeting as part of a monologue to which the claimant did not respond. He had a particular example in mind: it related to the events of the morning of 25 October. As I have already described, that was due to a shortage of kitchen staff. It demonstrated that the claimant was aware of different options that he had when there was a shortage of staff in a particular area. It did not, however demonstrate awareness on the claimant's part that there always had to be a manager present on the premises.

From Judge Horne's written reasons for the Judgment. Contrary to what Judge Horne states here, Mr Frodsham relied on the 24 Oct 2014 and a Manager absence, it's clearly written in the dismissal letter (see 'Image 016b').

It was Mr Krohn who relied on a kitchen staff absence, on 25 Oct 2014, to uphold the dismissal (as confirmed later in fraud 17). Mr Frodsham stated at Tribunal that he only became aware of the alleged Oct 2014 incident sometime AFTER the disciplinary hearing had ended; therefore he could NOT have had it in mind during the Disciplinary Hearing itself and, by not putting this specific incident to Claimant at that meeting, Mr Frodsham denied Claimant a fair opportunity to meet that argument.

Image 016b

> On your final point, you have admitted that you would in similar circumstances again, phone rather than email. I refer at this point to an instance on 24th October 2014 where in fact you did by your own actions acknowledge the need for sufficient appointed managerial cover on site by extending your own shift period to 09:45 to cover a managerial staff shortage having made appropriate telephone contact with relevant staff members to advise of the problem.

From the Dismissal Letter written by Mr Frodsham; he clearly states it was 'managerial cover' on '24th October 2014'. It had never been investigated or established prior to dismissal that this specific 'occasion' had occurred, yet Mr Frodsham still relied on it to dismiss Claimant, then subsequently relied on it at Employment Tribunal even after it had been established that the Claimant was not at work on that occasion.

Image 016c

> 15. The Respondent considered all the information and concluded that the Claimant had committed an act of misconduct, as it was clear for the way the Claimant had acted that he knew his actions could cause problems. Also the Claimant had not acted in this way previously, when a similar circumstance had arisen.

From Employer's ET3 Form. Peninsula/Employer state there was 'a similar circumstance' to the 02 Jan 2015 incident that Claimant previously dealt with i.e. Manager absence cover.

The only Manager absence cover cited by Employer was the one Mr Frodsham used in the Dismissal letter; an incident which at the time of dismissal had never been established as taking place but, was established as NOT taking place by the time Peninsula/Employer completed the ET3 Form (see fraud 17).

Image 016d

> 55. I was confident that James knew that there needed to be a duty manager on the premises at all times because he had stayed late himself on one occasion in October.

From Mr Frodsham's written statement of 'FACT' to the Employment Tribunal – Mr Frodsham states that Claimant 'stayed late himself on one occasion in October'. The only occasion ever cited by Mr Frodsham was Claimant staying over on 24 Oct 2014 to cover for a Manager absence; therefore he can only be referring to that occasion. However, by the time Mr Frodsham wrote his statement of 'FACT' to the ET, that occasion had been established as NOT taking place (see fraud 17).

Image 016e

> Common sense would dictate that you try to find another manager to cover or you stay yourself until someone can relieve you. James knew this, because he did exactly that in October.

From Mr Frodsham's written statement of 'FACT' to the Employment Tribunal. As Claimant ONLY 'stayed late himself on one occasion in October', Mr Frodsham stating 'He did exactly that in October' demonstrates he is referring to that 'one occasion' i.e. Claimant covering for a Manager absence. However, by the time Mr Frodsham wrote his statement of 'FACT' to the ET, that 'one occasion' had been established as NOT taking place (see fraud 17).

Image 016f

> James could have stayed himself, as he had in October. He didn't.

From Mr Frodsham's written statement of 'FACT' to the Employment Tribunal. Mr Frodsham once more relying on the 'one occasion in October' when Claimant stayed late to cover for an absent Manager; an occasion that, by the time Mr Frodsham wrote his statement of 'FACT' to the ET, had been established as NOT taking place (see fraud 17).

Image 016g

> In respect of the comparison to the October incident when he did facilitate arrangements - advised to check dates and be able to confirm this happened (even if wrong date was given in original outcome letter).
>
> Advised to take detailed notes, we know he will challenge them - don't get into discussion about previous warning, that's been done and this appeal is only for the current issue of misconduct.
> 09/03/2015 17:03

Communication between Employer and Peninsula – prior to the Disciplinary Appeal Hearing. The 'October incident' was relied on to dismiss the Claimant; ONLY NOW, just over a month after Claimant's dismissal, do Peninsula think it might be a good idea to confirm if the incident actually occurred.

Image 016h

Additionally – we also need to clear up the issue around the 25th October – what actually happened that day please, it isn't clear to me now if we can use this as an example of him ensuring to leave the hotel with sufficient appointed management cover by taking appropriate action?

16/03/2015 17:20

Communication between Employer and Peninsula – after the Disciplinary Appeal Hearing. Peninsula again ask for some clarity on the October issue; which now demonstrates that Claimant was dismissed without this issue first being 'carefully investigated', or the facts being established and put to Claimant, which breached Employer's own Disciplinary Procedures (there is some confusion with the date as Employer relied on a Manager absence cover on 24 Oct to dismiss Claimant).

Image 016i

From: Kim Eivind Krohn
Sent: 16 March 2015 22:19
To: Steven Frodsham
Subject: Fwd: LIG035 - Private & Confidential

Fyi

Can you see if you can get some points together as i will not have time until i get back and i am worried that we have waisted enought time on the notes i had to retype

K

Additionally – we also need to clear up the issue around the 25th October – what actually happened that day please, it isn't clear to me now if we can use this as an example of him ensuring to leave the hotel with sufficient appointed management cover by taking appropriate action? - I don't think this can be used now, the date in question he is correct in saying that he was off the night shift of 24th October, so would not have been present in the building on the morning of 25th October.

Kind regards

Communication between Mr Krohn (Appeal Officer) and Mr Frodsham (Disciplinary Officer) – after the Disciplinary Appeal. Mr Krohn repeats Peninsula's message to Mr

Frodsham and asks him what actually happened on the day in question (again, some confusion with the date but, as Mr Frodsham relied on the issue to dismiss Claimant, he will know what Mr Krohn is referring to). As you can see, Employer now confirms that Claimant wasn't in work on the morning in question; now demonstrating that Employer relied on an incident, which Claimant had no involvement with, to dismiss him.

Image 016j

> Hello Kim
>
> Thanks for this - the issue of 25th October is quite key though, as it demonstrated awareness he knew he had to source cover. If we let this go now we fundamentally weaken our case. I need you/ Steven to get the detail on this - why did we rely on it at all if it didn't happen please?
>
> I'll look to start drafting the outcome letter next week based on your summary statement and the information provided. If you could please drill down into this October incident though.
>
> 20/03/2015 17:17

Communication between Employer and Peninsula – Peninsula, the so called 'experts' in Employment Law, have now been made aware that Claimant was dismissed by relying on an incident he wasn't involved with. Peninsula directs Employer to 'get the detail on this'; which is something that should have been done before relying on the issue to dismiss Claimant and again demonstrates Employer breached their own procedures by NOT 'carefully investigating' the facts before sanctioning Claimant.

Image 016k

> 16. The claimant does not agree with paragraph 49 of the Reasons, and takes issue in particular with my finding that Mr Frodsham had the example of 25 October 2014 in mind at the time of the reconvened disciplinary meeting. Whether that finding is correct or not, it is clear that Mr Frodsham had that example in mind by the time he wrote the dismissal letter. There is no prospect of my finding that Mr Frodsham did not take it into account in reaching his decision to dismiss.

From Judge Horne's first written refusal to reconsider the Judgment. Claimant had argued that, as Mr Frodsham *admitted to only finding out about the Oct 2014 issue <u>after</u> the Disciplinary Hearing had finished, it was not investigated, it was not put to Claimant during the hearing, Claimant was denied a fair opportunity to meet the argument, and more importantly Mr Frodsham could not have had it in mind <u>during</u> the Disciplinary Hearing.*

Further, Mr Frodsham had the 24 October 2014 in mind, NOT the 25; he clearly states that in the dismissal letter. Regardless of which of those dates it was, the fact that Mr Frodsham 'took it into account in reaching his decision to dismiss' demonstrates he breached Employment Law i.e. 'O'Farrill v New Manage Ltd t/a Hooks Gym London Shootfighters', by imposing a sanction in respect of an allegation that was NOT investigated and NOT brought to the Claimant's attention as part of the proceedings.

17. **Peninsula/Employer put to Employment Tribunal, or inferred, that on the morning of 25 Oct 2014 Claimant WAS in charge when an unforeseen kitchen staff absence occurred and that Claimant made a *'Management decision'* to stay over after his shift had ended because *'NO suitable staff member was present to cover the absence'* (see 'Image 017a' and 'Image 017b'); a supposed awareness was then drawn out that *'Claimant's decision'* to stay over in 2014 while he was in charge regarding a kitchen staff absence meant he knew to stay over on 02 Jan 2015 when it was a Manager absence – however, undisclosed *evidence (see 'Image 017c' to 'Image 017f')* demonstrates that this was a conscious and deliberate dishonesty as another Manager WAS on duty and HAD taken charge of the hotel on 25 Oct 2014. More importantly, there was no unforeseen kitchen**

staff absence that morning which needed to be dealt with; in fact, the official report of the day *(see 'Image 017g')* documents that Claimant stayed over because the staff put on shift by the Employer were NOT trained to do the jobs they were put there for i.e. they couldn't cook breakfast for the guests, and none of them could cover reception while the GSM on duty cooked breakfast.

Also, the fact that, at Employment Tribunal, Employer had to draw out a supposed awareness on Claimant's part, rather than disclosing documented evidence to establish they had informed him of specific conditions procedures and rules, again demonstrates that Employer had NOT made those things known to Claimant *(which is now very relevant to fraud 15).*

Further, the alleged kitchen staff absence had no supporting investigation notes, was NOT put to Claimant during the Disciplinary Hearing, was not relied on to dismiss Claimant, nor was it put to Claimant during the Appeal Hearing; it was simply relied on to uphold the dismissal in the Appeal Outcome letter therefore, Claimant was not given a fair opportunity to meet this argument before the dismissal was upheld.

The fact that Mr Krohn took this issue into account when reaching his decision to uphold the dismissal demonstrates he too breached Employment Law i.e. *'O'Farrill v New Manage Ltd t/a Hooks Gym London Shootfighters'*, by imposing a sanction in respect of an allegation that was NOT investigated and NOT brought to the Claimant's attention as part of the proceedings. This too is relevant to previous fraud 14.

Image 017a

> Of particular importance, in my opinion, was the fact that a similar incident had happened on 25 October 2015 and James had taken it upon himself to work additional hours so that there would be no staff shortage on the busy morning shift. I explain this at the top of **page 171**.

From Mr Krohn's (Appeal Officer) statement of 'FACT' to the Employment Tribunal. According to Mr Krohn, the 25 Oct was 'Of particular importance' when he made the decision to uphold Claimant's dismissal because it was concerning a 'similar incident' to the one faced by Claimant on 02 Jan 2015 i.e. 'Manager' absence cover. However, by the time Mr Krohn wrote this statement to the ET, the issue of Claimant covering for a Manager absence in October 2014 had been established as NOT taking place (as demonstrated here and in fraud 16).

Image 017b

> Having investigated the incidents of 25th October 2014, it has been found that you had covered until 9.45am for a kitchen staff member who had reported their absence earlier in your shift. You subsequently acknowledged the need for action to deal with this absence and took this upon yourself to arrange and ensure that there would be no staff shortage during the busy breakfast shift. You contacted Kristian who you told that you had covered and you were leaving so he had to be contactable in his room in the hotel. This demonstrates that as a duty manager you were well aware of what the procedure was to arrange cover for gaps in operational staffing levels. This then raises questions as to why you did not feel it necessary to follow this same procedure on 2nd January 2015 when the hotel was left without an appointed person. On this particular occasion, the fact that it was a more senior staff member that would be absent only increases your obligation and duty to facilitate an arrangement to cover – either by staying on yourself or by telephoning to communicate the staff shortfall. On 25th October 2015 you identified that no suitable staff member was present to cover the absence, acted on this by remaining yourself, and then took it upon yourself to contact a staff member who was suitable for the purpose at hand. I therefore find, on the balance of probabilities, that your actions on 2nd January 2015 were a wilful dereliction of a known or appreciated duty on your part which left the hotel at risk.

From the Court Bundle 'the top of page 171' – which was a copy of the Appeal Outcome Letter from Mr Krohn. Apparently there was an incident on 25 Oct 2014 which was investigated; an incident that was never documented in any investigation notes and was never put to Claimant during the Disciplinary or Appeal hearings, thereby denying Claimant a fair opportunity to meet the argument. According to Mr

Krohn, a 'kitchen staff member' had reported their absence during the Claimant's shift; however, for ET purposes, a 'kitchen staff member absence' is NOT 'a similar incident' to a 'Manager absence', which demonstrates that no 'similar incident' occurred and that Mr Krohn's statement to the ET on this issue was false and misleading.

Mr Krohn also uses the Appeal Outcome Letter to convince ET that Claimant was in charge at the time as 'no suitable staff member was present to cover the absence' i.e. no other 'Manager' was on site; however, long before Mr Krohn had written his statement of 'FACT' to the ET, he had established that there was another Manager on site (see 'Image 017d') who was in charge as she had relieved Claimant of that responsibility when her shift started at 7am.

Image 017c

Hello Kim

Apologies I've not been available... In respect of the further information about the 25th October, I am concerned this isn't now as strong as what we first thought.

We need this incident to demonstrate 'like for like' - ie, that James was in charge when a situation arose that meant the hotel would be left with "insufficient, appointed management cover" - and that he subsequently took steps to avoid that happening.

The situation you've described as 'someone from the kitchen' - was that someone who would have been taking over the management/ GSM duties?

23/03/2015 20:23

Communication between Employer and Peninsula – it seems that, after establishing Claimant was dismissed because they relied on an incident which Claimant had no involvement with, Employer simply found a day when Claimant had stayed over and rewrote the narrative to make it fit with the dismissal. Employer then put that story to Peninsula; it's gone from Claimant covering for a 'Manager' absence on the 24

Oct, to Claimant covering for 'someone from the kitchen' on the 25 Oct.

Instead of Peninsula advising damage limitations by correcting the dismissal, they brush aside the fact that Employer dismissed Claimant by relying on an incident he was not involved with, and simply go along with the new narrative; Peninsula do point out that this new narrative does NOT demonstrate 'like for like' to the 'Manager' absence on 02 Jan 2015.

However, despite being informed the incident was NOT 'like with like', Mr Krohn still relied on this alleged incident as 'like with like' when upholding the dismissal (as seen in previous 'Image 017b') and further relied on it as 'like with like' in his statement of 'FACT' to the Employment Tribunal (see previous 'Image 017a').

Image 017d

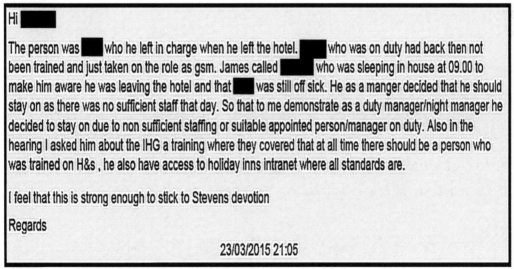

Hi ▮

The person was ▮ who he left in charge when he left the hotel. ▮ who was on duty had back then not been trained and just taken on the role as gsm. James called ▮ who was sleeping in house at 09.00 to make him aware he was leaving the hotel and that ▮ was still off sick. He as a manger decided that he should stay on as there was no sufficient staff that day. So that to me demonstrate as a duty manager/night manager he decided to stay on due to non sufficient staffing or suitable appointed person/manager on duty. Also in the hearing I asked him about the IHG a training where they covered that at all time there should be a person who was trained on H&s , he also have access to holiday inns intranet where all standards are.

I feel that this is strong enough to stick to Stevens devotion

Regards

23/03/2015 21:05

Communication between Employer and Peninsula.

Employer disclosed that another GSM WAS on duty 'back then' i.e. on the morning of 25 Oct 2014; which demonstrated

that, even though Claimant had stayed on site past the end of his shift, another GSM was in charge of the hotel and responsible for ALL management decisions as she had relieved Claimant of that responsibility when her shift started at 7am.

Employer also disclosed that the GSM on duty was NOT trained at the time; which now supports the Claimant's statement that NOT ALL Guest Service Managers were trained, and demonstrates that Peninsula/Employer misled the ET when they stated that ALL GSMs were trained.

If Employer had conducted a proper investigation they would have established that, on 25 Oct 2014, the untrained GSM asked Claimant to stay and support her because it was a busy morning with untrained kitchen staff and a wedding group to deal with; therefore, NOT a 'Management Decision' from Claimant, but a request from another GSM. Instead, Employer ran with a narrative that had not been investigated, or established, or documented anywhere.

There is reference to another person 'sleeping in house', but that person was NOT employed by the Employer; he was actually employed by a different company, at a different hotel, in a lower position than GSM, and was simply there to help out during the rebrand. Employer confirms 'there was no sufficient staff that day' despite this person sleeping in house.

Employer also disclosed that the Chef 'was still off sick' that morning; indicating that he was already off sick prior to that day. In fact, that one remark prompted a closer inspection of the staff rota disclosed to Employment Tribunal (see Image 017e), and it clearly shows the Chef was off sick that entire week and the entire previous week. After inspecting more rotas held by Claimant, it was found that the Chef had been off sick for the past 34 days (since 21 Sept 2014), demonstrating that his absence on the 35th day would be very likely, therefore NOT unforeseen; Employer failed to plan for the Chef's absence that morning and instead put untrained kitchen staff on shift with an untrained Manager.

Further, Employer states that Claimant stayed because there was no 'suitable appointed person/manager on duty' as a result of the Chef's absence; which demonstrates that there would have been no issue with 'suitable appointed person/manager on duty' had the Chef been on shift.

This is very relevant because we now know the GSM on duty wasn't trained, as admitted by Mr Krohn in 'Image 017d'; therefore, the fact that staffing would have been suitable had the Chef not been absent that morning demonstrates that the Chef must be better trained than the GSM on duty. That being the case, the Chef must also be suitable to be left in charge because the untrained 'manager on duty' was, by virtue of being a GSM, suitable to be left in charge.

The Employer couldn't have foreseen that Claimant would stay over that morning therefore, even if the Chef was not better trained than the GSM on duty, the mere fact that an untrained GSM was put on shift to be left in charge of the hotel by the Employer, demonstrates that Employer had no issues with untrained staff being left in charge. The ONLY time Employer had an issue with untrained staff being left in charge was when they needed to justify Claimant's dismissal.

Image 017e

	MON 13-Oct-14	TUE 14-Oct-14	WED 15-Oct-14	THU 16-Oct-14	FRI 17-Oct-14	SAT 18-Oct-14	SUN 19-Oct-14	MON 20-Oct-14	TUE 21-Oct-14	WED 22-Oct-14	THU 23-Oct-14	FRI 24-Oct-14	SAT 25-Oct-14	SUN 26-Oct-14
Conf	s/wiches		hot buffet	hot buffet					breakfast	hot buffet			wedding	
Groups					3 x dbb	3 x dbb	1 x dbb	1 x dbb	1 x dbb			1 x dbb	2 x dbb	1 x bb / 1 x dbb
Steven	IN	IN	IN	IN	IN	IN	OFF	IN	IN	IN	IN			
Charlie	Light	Light	OFF	EARLY	Late	Late	Early	OFF	Light	Light	OFF	Late	Late	Early
Guest Service Managers														
	OFF	OFF	Late	Late	Late	Late	Early	Late	Late	Late	Late	Late	Early	OFF
	Early	Early	Early	Early	Early	OFF	OFF	Early	Early	Early	Early	Early	OFF	OFF
	Late	Late	Early	OFF	OFF	OFF	Late	Hol	Hol	Hol	Hol	Hol	Hol	Hol
	OFF	OFF	OFF	Late	Late	Early	Early	OFF	Late	OFF	Late	Late	16.00-00.00	EARLY
Guest Service Assistants														
	07.00-15.00	07.00-15.00	07.00-15.00	OFF	07.00-11.00	OFF	OFF	07.00-15.00	07.00-15.00	07.00-15.00	OFF	07.00-11.00	OFF	OFF
	OFF	OFF	OFF	OFF	OFF	17.00-22.00	07.00-12.00	OFF	OFF	OFF	OFF	OFF	Split	Split
	07.00-11.00	07.00-11.00	OFF	OFF	Late	OFF	OFF	Hol	OFF	OFF	OFF	OFF	OFF	OFF
	OFF	OFF	OFF	OFF	18.00-22.00	17.00-22.00	07.00-12.00	Split	OFF	18.00-22.00	07.00-11.00	OFF	17.00-01.00	08.00-12.00
	18.00-22.00	18.00-22.00	OFF	07.00-15.00	OFF	18.00-22.00	18.00-22.00	Split	07.00-11.00	07.00-11.00	07.00-11.00	18.00-22.00	OFF	OFF
	Late	Late	Late	Late	Early	Early	OFF	Late	Late	Late	OFF	07.00-15.00	OFF	07.00-15.00
	OFF	OFF	18.00-22.00	18.00-22.00	OFF	07.00-11.00	Late	18.00-22.00	18.00-22.00	18.00-22.00	18.00-22.00	OFF	16.00-00.00	Late
Nights														
	OFF	OFF	NIGHT	NIGHT	NIGHT	NIGHT	NIGHT	NIGHT	NIGHT	OFF	OFF	NIGHT	NIGHT	OFF
	NIGHT	NIGHT	OFF	OFF	NIGHT	NIGHT	NIGHT	NIGHT	NIGHT	NIGHT	NIGHT	NIGHT	18.00-01.00	OFF
	NIGHT	NIGHT	NIGHT	NIGHT	OFF	OFF	OFF	OFF	18.00-22.00	NIGHT	NIGHT	OFF	NIGHT	NIGHT
James	18.00-22.00	18.00-22.00	18.00-22.00	OFF	18.00-22.00	18.00-22.00	OFF	18.00-22.00	18.00-22.00	18.00-22.00	OFF	18.00-22.00	18.00-22.00	OFF
Kitchen														
	SICK	SICK	SICK	OFF	SICK	SICK	SICK	OFF	SICK	SICK	SICK	SICK	SICK	SICK
CHEF	EARLY	LATE	NIGHT	OFF	IN	HOL	18.00-22.00	17 - 22	12.00-20.00 / 18.00-23.00	18.00-23.00	AFD	Split	10.00-18.00	Course
SPLIT														

Rota for 13 Oct 2014 – 26 Oct 2014 as disclosed to Employment Tribunal (we have identified the Chef for this publication).

It also has to be noted here that the Chef being off sick was never put to Claimant during the Disciplinary or Appeal Hearings therefore Claimant was not given a fair chance to meet that argument during the Disciplinary Process.

Image 017f

> In my opinion, there was no sufficient staffing in place: ▓▓▓▓▓ was not an appropriate person to leave in charge

From Mr Krohn's statement of 'Fact' to the Employment Tribunal regarding 02 Jan 2015. After stating to Peninsula that in 2014 the Chef was better trained and more suitable than a GSM (see previous 'Image 017d'), Mr Krohn subsequently told Employment Tribunal that in 2015 the Chef was less suitable and less trained than a GSM.

In 2014 Employer needed the Chef to be more suitable and better trained in order for his absence to cause an insufficiency of staff, but in 2015 Employer needed the Chef to be less suitable and less trained than a GSM in order to justify Claimant's dismissal. This demonstrates that the Chef's suitability was solely dependent on what argument Employer was putting forward at a given time.

At no point in any of the documented discussions between Peninsula and Employer was the Chef's 'drinking problem' mentioned; therefore, Employer didn't see the Chef's drinking problem as an issue, and it was NOT relied on to Dismiss Claimant or uphold the Dismissal. The Chef's 'drinking problem' was ONLY disclosed verbally at Employment Tribunal when Employer wanted to reinforce their reason as to why the Chef was not appropriate to be left in charge of the hotel.

While it did reinforce that reason, it opened up other issues that were overlooked at Tribunal such as 'Health & Safety' being put at risk by Employer leaving the Chef unmanaged, in charge of the most dangerous part of the hotel, when they knew he had a drinking problem.

Image 017g

Nights	
Duty Manager (s)	James
Resort Appearance	
Staffing	On a busy breakfast like today (Sat morn) we need at least one experienced member of staff in the kitchen to take over the cooking or, someone who can cover the desk so the GSM can get in the kitchen. There was none today which is why I ended up stayin till 9am. JB

From Duty Manager Report for the night of 24 going into 25 Oct 2014. Claimant stayed over on the 25 Oct because the kitchen staff on duty were NOT trained to take over the cooking, and none of them could cover reception so the GSM could take over the cooking. The Duty Manager Report for 24/25 Oct 2014 was disclosed to Employment Tribunal but Peninsula/Employer convinced Judge Horne that the entry in question was regarding a staff absence; even when Claimant stated during cross examination that the staff put on shift by the Employer were not trained, the consultant for Peninsula responded with 'so, a staff absence', implying that 'untrained staff on duty' and 'a staff absence' were the same thing.

It is clear from the new evidence that it was a conscious and deliberate dishonesty when Peninsula/Employer cited the alleged 24 and 25 Oct 2014 incidents in their ET3 Form, and more so each time they subsequently relied on, or referred to, those alleged incidents during the Employment Tribunal.

18. Peninsula/Employer put to Employment Tribunal, or inferred, that Claimant KNEW there had to be a Manager on site at ALL TIMES – however, undisclosed evidence *(see 'Image 018')* demonstrates that this was a conscious and deliberate dishonesty as Peninsula/Employer had, prior to the dismissal, established that Claimant would NOT have seen a document which stated a Guest Services Manager had to be on site for the 16 hours between 7am and 11pm.

Image 018

There is a document that says need GSM between 7-11, however JB won't have seen this.

22/01/2015 20:50

Communication between Employer and Peninsula – prior to dismissal. As the document cited refers to a 'GSM', it can only be in relation to the franchise agreement as the role of GSM was an IHG designation and didn't exist prior to that agreement coming into force.

It's now looking more likely that Claimant didn't know there had to be a Manager on site at 'ALL times' because:-

    I.   *there wasn't always a Manager on site during the night for the 4 years when Claimant was in a non-management position as a Night Porter prior to TUPE – a fact Claimant personally knew from his own knowledge and experience and one which Employer had NO 'Reasonable Grounds' to disbelieve as different hotel brands had different policies regarding Managers and, Employer failed to establish the policies of the previous owners.*

    II.   *Employer admitted that, prior to the rebrand, THEY*

had no written procedures in place stating that Managers had to be on site at all times; thereby confirming that different hotel brands had different policies regarding Managers.

    III.   *Employer only 'thinks' there MAY have been IHG training with information about managers being on site – but it was never established that there was any such training or that Claimant had attended it.*

    IV.   *And now we have confirmation that Claimant wouldn't have seen a relevant IHG document that stated Managers had to be on site between 7am and 11pm.*

'Image 018' now demonstrates that whenever Peninsula/Employer stated 'at all times' for ET purposes, in relation to Claimant knowing when there HAD to be Managers on site, they were misleading the Tribunal as they didn't actually mean at 'ALL' times because they knew Claimant hadn't been informed that Managers had to be on site for the 16 hours between 7am and 11pm.

19. **Employer put to Employment Tribunal, or inferred, that ALL GSMs *(Guest Service Managers)*, and ALL Night Staff, HAD done *'Advanced'* First Aid Training by 01 Oct 2014; Employer maintained that this training was required before staff could be left in charge of the hotel and that lack of this training put Health & Safety at risk** – however, undisclosed evidence *(see 'Image 019a' and 'Image 019b')* demonstrates that this was a conscious and deliberate dishonesty as Employer was fully aware that certain GSMs and Night Staff

only did this training in mid Jan 2015 yet, Employer deemed them as suitable to cover the Manager absence on 02 Jan 2015 *(see 'Image 019c' and 'Image 019d')* despite them NOT being trained to the required standard; which again *(as in previous fraud 17)* demonstrates that Employer themselves had no problem with putting untrained staff in charge of the hotel and, that lack of *'Advanced'* First Aid Training only became an issue when they needed to justify Claimant's dismissal.

Image 019a

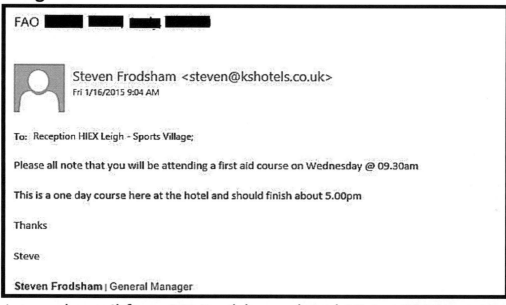

FAO ■■■ ■■■ ■■■ ■■■■

Steven Frodsham <steven@kshotels.co.uk>
Fri 1/16/2015 9:04 AM

To: Reception HIEX Leigh - Sports Village;

Please all note that you will be attending a first aid course on Wednesday @ 09.30am

This is a one day course here at the hotel and should finish about 5.00pm

Thanks

Steve

Steven Frodsham | General Manager

Internal email from Mr Frodsham, dated 16 Jan 2015, sent to several GSMs and 1 Night Staff informing them that they will be attending a first aid course; during the Employment Tribunal this training will be referred to as 'Additional', 'Advanced' or 'Enhanced' First Aid Training.

According to Employer at ET, there were two lots of training that IHG (Intercontinental Hotels Group) required hotel staff to complete before they could be left in charge of the hotel; 'Advanced Fire Safety Training' and 'Advanced First Aid

Training'. Failure to do either one meant you were not trained to the required standard and 'Health & Safety' of the hotel would be put at risk if you were left in charge; which is the argument Employer used regarding the cover staff not having this training.

Yet, ALL 4 of the staff named in the email were deemed suitable to cover the Manager absence on 02 Jan 2015 despite them NOT being trained to the required standard; a standard which Employer applied to the cover staff in order to dismiss Claimant.

Image 019b

Holiday Inn Express Leigh – GSM Meeting

Meeting called to order at 3.00pm on 16/01/15 by Steven Frodsham (GM).

Members Present:

Steven Frodsham
Charlie Brimacombe
██████████
██████████
██████████

Business – (Start 15.25)

- ██████████ has been promoted to Reservations Manager and he would like to let all staff know he is there if they need him and try not to go to ████.
- ████████ and ██████ have now left the Company
- ██████ has stepped up in his Supervisor role, but could do with a little support on the computer.
- ██████ considering full time hours.
- First Aid Training scheduled for Wednesday 21st January for ████, ████, ████, ████, ████ plus 5 from the Light

From a management meeting held on 16 Jan 2015 to discuss various issues at the hotel. The meeting was chaired by Mr Frodsham (Disciplinary Officer) and attended by Mr Brimacombe (Investigation Officer); Claimant was never invited to this meeting or given a copy of the notes.

One of the items raised was confirmation of First Aid Training. Although the training was not a mandatory legal requirement, the Employer relied on it to justify Claimant's dismissal; in doing so, Employer told the Tribunal that this training was completed by ALL Managers and ALL Night Staff prior to 01 Oct 2014.

Now we have documented confirmation that Peninsula/ Employer misled the Tribunal because, prior to completing the training in Jan 2015, these Managers and Night Staff were not of the required standard to be left in charge.

You will also notice there is mention of a 'Supervisor'; the job title which Peninsula/Employer claimed at Tribunal was changed to GSM in Oct 2014 due to new terminology from the franchise agreement.

Image 019c

> C:- But Steve sleeps over , myself , ███ & ███ have all slept over

From Mr Brimacombe's 2015 'Investigation Notes'. Despite one of the named staff not being trained to the required standard i.e. they had to attend the First Aid training course as mentioned in 'Image 019a' and 'Image 019b', Mr Brimacombe lists him amongst the staff suitable to sleep over when Claimant is off work.

Image 019d

> C:- Why not call myself , ███ , ███ , ███ , ███ ?

From Mr Brimacombe's 2015 'Investigation Notes'. Despite two of the named staff not being trained to the required standard i.e. they had to attend the First Aid training course as mentioned in 'Image 019a' and 'Image 019b', Mr Brimacombe lists them amongst the staff Claimant could have called to cover the Manager absence and take charge of the hotel.

Let's not forget that, in order to justify Claimant's dismissal at Employment Tribunal, the Employer relied on the cover staff not having done the required training. Now we have evidence that Employer knew the staff they left in charge, or deemed sufficient to be left in charge, had also not done the required training.

As a side note, at no point during the investigation did Mr Brimacombe mention, or rely on, the other Night Staff being suitably trained to be left in charge of the hotel when Claimant was off work; Mr Brimacombe simply relied on other staff sleeping in on those nights. However, IF the other Night Staff were trained to the required standard, as Employer had the Tribunal believe, there would have been no need to have other staff sleep in when Claimant was off work.

20. **Peninsula/Employer put to Employment Tribunal, or inferred, that Claimant HAD done the required 'Advanced Fire Safety' training therefore he was sufficient to be left in charge, but that the cover staff had not done the required training and leaving them in charge was a risk to Health & Safety** – however, undisclosed evidence *(see 'Image 020a' to 'Image 020g')* demonstrates that this was a conscious and deliberate dishonesty as a Fire Risk Assessment carried out by Peninsula in Sept 2014 confirms that NO STAFF had done *'advanced'* Fire Safety Training prior to Sept 2014.

Attending a training session wasn't enough to be considered as trained when it came to *'Advanced Fire Safety'*; to be trained you had to pass an assessment at the end of the session, then be issued with a certificate of proof that would be filed in your training record and a copy placed in the hotel's Fire Safety File.

Despite Peninsula advising businesses in general to make sure they have a *'paper trail of defense with ongoing training, guidence, supervision and instruction'*, and despite IHG Brand Standards demanding that *'Documented evidence of completed training must be maintained'*, and despite a Disclosure Order being in place from Judge Horne for ALL relevant documents, Employer failed to disclose any *'paper trail of defense'* such as training records or certificates to support that Claimant had completed *'Advanced Fire Safety training'* after Sept 2014. Employer disclosed documents for the legally required mandatory training which all staff had done, and which was not in question or relied on to dismiss Claimant; but the training Employer relied on to dismiss Claimant had NO supporting documents.

In fact, at Employment Tribunal, Mr Krohn *(Appeal Officer)* stated that the other Night Staff, who Employer claimed were trained to the correct standard, were better trained than Claimant because Claimant didn't do the training. Claimant subsequently pointed this out in his letter to Judge Horne requesting a reconsideration of the judgment; to which Judge Horne cited *'context'* in his refusal letter *(see Image 020h)*. However, we now know the context put forward by Employer at Tribunal, and relied on by Judge Horne, was not the context at the time of dismissal.

Regardless of *'context'*, when it came to training standards, either they had to be met in which case Employer by their own admission put *'Health & Safety'* at risk when leaving Claimant in charge knowing he wasn't correctly trained, or training standards didn't have to be met in which case there should have been no issue with Claimant leaving the cover staff in charge. Again, Employer themselves had no problem with putting untrained staff in charge of the hotel; lack of *'Advanced Fire Safety training'* only became an issue when Peninsula/Employer needed to justify Claimant's dismissal at ET.

Image 020a

4. FIRE EXTINGUISHERS	Compliant	Part Compliant	Non Compliant	N/A
Have staff had training in the use of fire extinguishers?			x	
5. MANAGEMENT AND PROCEDURES	Compliant	Part Compliant	Non Compliant	N/A
Has an emergency plan been drawn up in case of fire?	✓			
Are all staff fully trained in this procedure?			x	

From 'Fire Risk Assessment' report that Peninsula created in Sept 2014 after conducting the assessment; the report was given to the Employer in order for them to action any recommendations. The report was a relevant document as it reviewed the hotel's Fire Safety files from the day of the report, to as far back as 2012 under the previous owners; any Fire Safety training that HAD been conducted prior to Sept 2014 would be documented within those Fire Safety files. This meant that, even without staff training records, Fire Training itself from Employer and the previous owners would be documented in a second place.

In 'Image 020a' Peninsula found that, in Sept 2014, the Employer had a Fire Evacuation plan in place but NONE of the staff were trained on it.

Image 020b

10. DOCUMENTATION AND RECORDS	Compliant	Part Compliant	Non Compliant	N/A	Comments / Recommendations
Are staff training records kept?			x		None viewed.

From 'Fire Risk Assessment' report that Peninsula created in Sept 2014. Peninsula found that, in Sept 2014, the Employer was 'non compliant' when it came to keeping training records. The fact that no training records were kept prior to Sept 2014 and no training was recorded in the hotel's Fire Safety files, together with the fact that this training was not an internal requirement for every hotel brand or a legal requirement, demonstrates that Employer had NO reasonable grounds to believe Claimant had done any additional fire training prior to them taking over the hotel when it was operated under a different brand.

Image 020c

12. GENERAL ISSUES	Compliant	Part Compliant	Non Compliant	N/A	Comments / Recommendations
Has responsible person received Fire Warden training?			x		No formal fire warden training has been carried out.

From 'Fire Risk Assessment' report that Peninsula created in Sept 2014. Peninsula found that, in Sept 2014, NO 'Responsible Person' had done formal Fire Warden Training (also referred to as advanced, enhanced, additional, or Fire Marshal training). This, together with the fact that no training records were kept prior to Sept 2014, and the fact that NO records were ever disclosed to establish that Claimant had completed such training after Sept 2014, ought to have cast doubt on Claimant's training; and probably would have done if Peninsula/Employer had not withheld the 'Fire Risk Assessment' report from Employment Tribunal.

Image 020d

4. Portable Fire Fighting Equipment
Fire extinguisher and fire warden training should be carried out for relevant persons within the Hotel.

From 'Fire Risk Assessment' report that Peninsula created in Sept 2014. Peninsula recommended Fire Warden Training. Yet again, at Employment Tribunal, and in response to Claimant's Subject Access Request, the Employer failed to disclose any records to support that Claimant had completed Fire Warden Training after Sept 2014. These were records that WOULD exist if Claimant had done such training, and documents which Employment Tribunal had ordered be disclosed.

Image 020e

5. Management and Procedures
It is proposed that the hotel are to have in place 'Fire Teams' and make use of flash cards within the emergency box which have been strategically placed for easy access, a systems has been developed whereby two differing arrangements are documented to deal with emergency's for varying levels of staff, however no training was viewed on such procedures.

From 'Fire Risk Assessment' report that Peninsula created in Sept 2014. Peninsula proposed that Employer puts 'Fire Teams' in place; demonstrating that no such teams existed on, or prior to, Sept 2014. Peninsula also confirmed that there is an Emergency System in place but that there was NO records to view that showed staff had been trained on the system.

Image 020f

6. Staff Training
It was noted there is a lack of fire training throughout the Hotel staff, see recommendations. All members of staff should receive in house training which should be recorded via a training matrix to assist in the review process.

From 'Fire Risk Assessment' report that Peninsula created in Sept 2014. Peninsula uncover a 'lack of fire training throughout the hotel' and recommend staff training be done and 'recorded via a training matrix'; yet, despite being advised to keep records, NO records to support that Claimant had completed any additional Fire Safety Training after Sept 2014 were disclosed in response to Claimant's Subject Access Request, or to the Employment Tribunal despite a disclosure order being in place. These were records that WOULD exist and would now be 'recorded via a training matrix' if Claimant had done such training.

Image 020g

Recommendations	Priority Rating H/M/L	Action carried out by	Completion
Fire extinguishers and fire marshal training should be carried out by relevant staff within the Hotel.	H		

From 'Fire Risk Assessment' report that Peninsula created in Sept 2014. Peninsula again recommended Fire Marshal (Warden) training but, this time, Peninsula marked it as a 'High Priority'. As it was a 'High Priority', you'd have thought Employer would be concerned enough to monitor it and ensure that this specific recommendation was carried out; but once more, at Employment Tribunal, and in response to Claimant's Subject Access Request, the Employer failed to disclose any records to support that Claimant had completed Fire Marshal Training after Sept 2014. These were training records that WOULD exist if Claimant had done such training, and documents which Employment Tribunal had ordered be disclosed.

The Fire Safety Assessment report created by Peninsula in Sept 2014 was very relevant as it found that NO ONE had done 'Advanced Fire Safety training' prior to Sept 2014; which demonstrates that Employer had no reasonable grounds to believe Claimant or anyone else had done such training with the previous owners. Employer would now have to show that THEY trained the Claimant at some point in Sept 2014 because the training was allegedly completed by 01 Oct 2014; yet, Peninsula/Employer failed to disclose the Fire Safety Assessment report to the Employment Tribunal and instead put forward, or inferred, that they 'believed' Claimant was trained under the previous owners.

On training in general, every company has a record of staff training; some as part of 'Due Diligence' and some as a legal requirement under 'Health & Safety'. It was therefore NOT reasonable of Employer to rely on a 'belief' of training in this instance because they had Claimant's training records and could establish as fact if he was trained or not.

Relying on a 'belief' demonstrated that either Employer hadn't bothered to check if Claimant was trained, or they had checked and found out he wasn't trained; whichever one it was also demonstrated that Employer took a risk with 'Health & Safety' each time they left Claimant alone and in charge of the hotel.

If records existed, supporting that Claimant had done 'Advanced Fire Safety' training, the Employer would have disclosed them at Disciplinary and Appeal stage, let alone at

Employment Tribunal. The failure of Employer to disclose such training records ought to have supported that Claimant was NOT trained, but it didn't; instead, Employer's groundless opinions were taken as 'beliefs' and therefore deemed as 'facts' by the Employment Tribunal.

Peninsula knew that NO ONE was trained prior to Sept 2014 because they conducted the assessment, they also knew Employer failed to keep training records prior to Sept 2014; yet Peninsula did not establish if such training had taken place after Sept 2014, and failed to establish if such training records were now kept. Instead, Peninsula allowed Employer to put forward to Tribunal that Claimant was trained by the previous owners.

If the Claimant leaving untrained staff in charge for just an hour was a genuine risk to 'Health & Safety' then, by that argument, the Employer leaving similarly untrained staff in charge from when they took over in June 2014 to Sept 2014 must also have been the same risk to Health & Safety; yet, Employer had NO concerns for the risk to Health & Safety posed by untrained staff prior to Sept 2014 – and it doesn't matter if Managers slept in prior to Sept 2014 as the 'Fire Risk Assessment' report established that NO ONE was trained.

As Claimant was left in charge of the hotel without him doing 'Advanced Fire Safety' training, it would also be reasonable of him NOT to have considered such training as a requirement when leaving the cover staff in charge.

Image 020h

I did take into account the fact that the claimant had denied having received the enhanced fire safety training (Reasons paragraph 42). I also bore in mind Mr Krohn's evidence that ███ and ███ had received more fire safety training than the claimant had, and that on the occasion when Mr Krohn attended for enhanced fire safety training, ███ and ███ were present but the claimant was not.

Mr Krohn's evidence had to be seen in the context of the evidence of the other witnesses. Mr Brimacombe's evidence was that the claimant had done the enhanced fire safety training. Mr Frodsham's evidence was that he believed that every GSM knew how to organise a fire evacuation, but that the three cover staff had not been trained in how to do it.

At the hearing the claimant relied on Mr Krohn's evidence to draw out a supposed inconsistency in treatment. The respondent was relying on the three cover staff's lack of training as a basis for concluding that it was misconduct for the claimant to leave three cover staff in charge of the hotel. At the same time, the respondent was content for other managers to leave the claimant in charge, despite the fact that (on Mr Krohn's evidence) the claimant had not had the same enhanced training as ███ and ███.

My view was, and remains, that the claimant was missing the point. The important consideration was not who had attended what training sessions. It was whether Mr Frodsham and Mr Krohn had reasonable grounds for believing that the three cover staff could not be relied on to organise a fire evacuation.

It was reasonable for the respondent to believe that the claimant, as a highly experienced GSM, knew how to organise a fire evacuation regardless of whether he had attended the same training session as ███ and ███ or indeed any training session under the new management regime. Mr Krohn did not say that he believed the claimant to be untrained in organising fire evacuations and it would have been surprising if he had. The claimant himself never suggested that he did not know how to organise a fire evacuation. The roles and duties of the three cover staff were entirely different to those of the claimant. It would be far less likely that their roles and duties would have led them to learn how to organise a fire evacuation. So it was highly relevant in their case that they had not received the enhanced fire safety training.

From Judge Horne's first written refusal to reconsider his decision.

At ET, Mr Krohn described an 'Advanced' training session he observed which the other Night Staff attended while Claimant was off work; Mr Krohn's evidence to Tribunal was that the other Night Staff 'had received more fire training than the

96

Claimant' and Mr Krohn stated directly to Judge Horne that the other Night Staff were 'better trained' than Claimant because Claimant hadn't done that training.

Without any clarification, Judge Horne deemed that Mr Krohn meant 'Claimant had not had the same enhanced training as the other Night Staff'; which implied Claimant had done different 'enhanced training'. As the Employer only had ONE form of 'enhanced fire training', and Claimant had not done that training, then any other 'enhanced fire training' must have come from the previous owners, and Employer let Tribunal believe that to be the case; but we now know that NO ONE did 'enhanced fire training' prior to Sept 2014. The mere fact that the other Night Staff were trained to the correct standard and, by Employer's own admission, were better trained than Claimant, demonstrates that Claimant was NOT trained to the correct standard and that Employer knew this and had no issue with Claimant not being trained when they left him in charge.

The 'context' at Tribunal was, the witnesses couldn't agree amongst themselves if Claimant was trained or not; one witness, Mr Brimacombe, stated that Claimant had done the 'enhanced' training, a second witness, Mr Frodsham, stated he 'believed' ALL GSMs had done the 'enhanced' training, and a third witness, Mr Krohn, stated Claimant had NOT done the 'enhanced' training. If 'Advanced Fire Safety training' was as vital to the hotel as Employer maintained it was, then they would know as 'fact' if Claimant was trained; for them not to know as 'fact' would be taking a risk with 'Health & Safety' each time they left Claimant alone and in charge of the hotel. Employer's witnesses contradicting each other on Claimant's training ought to have cast doubt on that training.

Mr Brimacombe's 'context' during the Disciplinary process was that he failed to disclose any alleged information he may have had regarding Claimant's training to the Claimant, or to Mr Frodsham, or to Mr Krohn; therefore Claimant had not been given a fair opportunity to meet this argument and it had no bearing on the decisions to dismiss Claimant or to uphold the dismissal.

It was 14 months later, at Employment Tribunal, when Mr Brimacombe first alleged Claimant had done the 'enhanced' training. But, had Claimant done this training, there would have been training records; which Employer failed to disclose. Also bear in mind that we now know Mr Brimacombe falsified 'Investigation Notes' and demonstrated he had no qualms in misleading the Employment Tribunal regarding those notes i.e. he put them forward to Employment Tribunal as complete and accurate 'investigation notes' when he knew they were not; therefore Mr Brimacombe would have no qualms in misleading the Tribunal regarding Claimant's training, especially as the Tribunal was accepting groundless opinions as fact.

Mr Brimacombe also had contempt for the Claimant, as demonstrated in 'Image 026f' of fraud 26, and contempt for the Tribunal, as demonstrated by the fact he mislead Judge Horne regarding investigation notes; which is more evidence that he would have no qualms in misleading the Tribunal regarding Claimant's training.

Mr Frodsham's 'context' during the Disciplinary process was that he knew NO ONE had done the training prior to Sept 2014, and he failed to establish if Claimant had done the training after that date; therefore, any 'belief' that '<u>every</u>

98

GSM knew how to organise a fire evacuation' was not reasonable simply because Mr Frodsham had no reasonable grounds to believe that Claimant, a GSM, had done the training.

The fact that, at ET, Mr Frodsham relied on a 'belief' at all, when he could very easily have verified training by checking training records, also demonstrates that Mr Frodsham breached the Disciplinary Procedures in place because the facts he relied on were not 'carefully investigated' before dismissing Claimant.

Peninsula's context *wasn't mentioned, so we'll tell you what it was; Peninsula was involved from the very start, was fully aware of the conversations they had with Employer regarding the Claimant, was aware of how Claimant had been dealt with, and knowingly went along with every piece of false information that Employer put to Employment Tribunal.*

When it comes to Claimant *not suggesting that he didn't know how to organise a fire evacuation, he was NEVER once asked if he did know; Employer just kept insisting that he did. However, Claimant did put to Employment Tribunal several times that he had NOT done 'enhanced fire safety training'; which Judge Horne acknowledges in 'Image 020h'. Since 'how to organise a fire evacuation' WAS part of the 'enhanced fire safety training', and because not having that training meant you wouldn't know 'how to organise a fire evacuation' e.g. the argument Employer was using in relation to the cover staff, then by definition of Claimant stating he had NOT done 'enhanced fire safety training' he WAS very much suggesting he didn't know 'how to organise a fire evacuation'. Let's not forget that Employer failed to disclose any records to show* *that Claimant had completed such training; records that would have existed IF Claimant had done this training, and records that Employment Tribunal ordered to be disclosed.*

As for the ET stating that 'The roles and duties of the three cover staff were entirely different to those of the claimant. It would be far less likely that their roles and duties would have led them to learn how to organise a fire evacuation. So it was highly relevant in their case that they had not received enhanced fire safety training'; this would likely be true under the previous owners when the hotel had different departments where staff roles and duties related to their specific department. However, when the Employer took over the hotel they merged all departments and, as stated by Mr Frodsham in his statement of 'FACT' to the Employment Tribunal, 'everyone is trained to do everything'. Also, in making their statement, the ET overlooked the fact that the Chef handled naked flames and gas in the kitchen therefore he was far more likely to have received 'enhanced fire safety training' because of that.

Whether or not Employer had reasonable grounds to believe the cover staff were not trained and would therefore not know how to 'organise a fire evacuation', they had no reasonable grounds to believe that Claimant was trained and would know how to 'organise a fire evacuation'; yet Employer still took a risk and left Claimant alone and in charge.

Therefore, Claimant was sanctioned for doing something which Employer regularly did i.e. leaving untrained staff in charge of the hotel. The only difference is, Claimant believed the cover staff were sufficiently trained, while Employer knew that Claimant was not sufficiently trained.

21. **Peninsula/Employer put to Employment Tribunal, or inferred, that leaving staff in charge who had not done *'advanced fire safety training'* PUT guest *'Health & Safety'* at risk as *'a fire evacuation would not run efficiently'* (see *'Image 021a'*) and *'a member of staff might cancel a fire alarm without properly evacuating the hotel, which would leave guests in danger'* (see *'Image 021b'*)** – however, as detailed in *'Image 017d'* of previous fraud 17, that was a conscious and deliberate dishonesty because Employer admitted to Peninsula that they themselves had put an untrained GSM on shift to be left in charge of the hotel on the morning of 25 Oct 2015; which demonstrates that Employer had NO concern that lack of *'advanced fire safety training'* would impact *'fire evacuation efficiency'* and *'Health & Safety'*, and had no concern that *'a member of staff might cancel a fire alarm without properly evacuating the hotel'*.

Further, as just detailed in fraud 20, we now know that NO STAFF had done *'advanced fire safety training'* under the previous owners, which demonstrates that this particular training was not a requirement of all hotel brands and that the basic Fire Safety training which ALL staff had done was sufficient for THIS hotel for over 5 years.

We also know that Employer themselves did not conduct *'advanced fire safety training'* for over 2 months, and only then in preparation for the hotel being re-branded, which demonstrates it was NOT a requirement of THIS hotel prior to getting ready for the re-branding and, that the basic Fire Safety training which ALL staff had done was sufficient until Sept 2014 *(or 25 Oct 2014 if you take into account the untrained GSM)* and again, Employer had NO concern that lack of *'advanced fire safety training'* would impact *'fire evacuation efficiency'* and *'Health & Safety'*, and had no concern that *'a member of staff might cancel a fire alarm without properly evacuating the hotel'*.

Not forgetting that Peninsula confirmed in the Fire Risk Assessment report created in Sept 2014 that the *'fire detection and warning system'* in place *'was adequate'* to *'alert occupants/guests to enable them to move away from the fire to a place of <u>total safety</u>' (see 'Image 021c')* and, *'Adequate means of escape are provided'* with *'Clear directional signage and emergency lighting' (see 'Image 021d')*. Therefore, the fire system in place was of such high standard that guests would still be able to evacuate to *'total safety'* without the need for staff supervision; which, considering Employer regularly left Claimant as the only member of staff on site through the night in charge of this four storey hotel with 135 rooms and several fire escape routes and exits around the building, was essential as Claimant could NOT be in all those places at once in a fire emergency.

While Claimant's actions MAY have breached IHG policy regarding Fire Safety Training *(we say 'may have' because Employer could not produce the IHG policy that was allegedly in force at the time, they could only produce the policy that came into force 6 months after Claimant's dismissal)*, a breach of such a policy was NOT a genuine risk to Health & Safety in this instance because the policy was internal, not a legal mandatory requirement, and lack of such a policy would NOT increase risk as demonstrated by the fact that risk did not increase when no such policy existed in the hotel for many years prior to the rebrand.

All mandatory legal *'fire safety'* requirements had been fulfilled by Claimant before he left the cover staff in charge and, as we now know, *'Health & Safety'* and *'fire evacuation efficiency'* was not seen as being put at risk on the 25 Oct 2014 when Employer left an untrained GSM in charge of the hotel, or for the 2 months prior to re-branding when NO STAFF had done *'advanced fire safety training',* or for the 5+ years under the previous owners when NO STAFF had done *'advanced fire safety training'.*

The fact that Employer relied on *'advanced Fire Safety Training'* at all demonstrates that they DID take *'IHG Brand Standards'* into account when dismissing Claimant; which is now relevant to fraud 31.

Image 021a

JB said: that the online training tells everyone how to evacuate guests so how is this putting the guests at risk?

SF said: so, not having a dedicated person to organise evacuation and how to operate the fire panel that would impact on the health and safety of guests – If there isn't anyone in charge on the day of an evacuation then this would not run efficiently and therefore would put the health and safety of guests in jeopardy.

From minutes of the Reconvened Disciplinary Hearing 2015.

Image 021b

A separate cohort of employees received additional fire safety training. This included how to organise a fire evacuation and how to operate the fire panel. There was nothing especially complicated about the fire panel, but the respondent reasonably took the view that the only people to be trained in its use were those who knew how to organise a fire evacuation. Otherwise, a member of staff might cancel a fire alarm without properly evacuating the hotel, which would leave guests in danger.

From Judge Horne's written reasons for the Judgment. Employer claims that staff without 'advanced' fire safety training 'might cancel the fire alarm without properly evacuating the hotel'; yet, Employer had no such concern on 25 Oct 2014 when the GSM who THEY put in charge was NOT trained, nor any concern prior to Sept 2014 when NONE of the staff had done 'advanced' fire safety training.

Image 021c

> The primary purpose of the Hotels automatic fire detection and warning system is to alert occupants/guests to enable them to move away from the fire to a place of total safety while the escape routes are still clear of smoke – upon viewing the system it was deemed as adequate.

From 'Fire Risk Assessment' report that Peninsula created in Sept 2014.

Image 021d

> Adequate means of escape are provided. Clear directional signage and emergency lighting are provided. Corridors are kept clear and adequate, compliant directional signage is provided leading to the exits.

From 'Fire Risk Assessment' report that Peninsula created in Sept 2014.

22. **Employer put to Employment Tribunal, or inferred, that the other Night Staff had done *'enhanced fire training'* prior to the Employer taking over the hotel** *(see 'Image 022a')* **and, that Claimant had told Mr Frodsham during the Disciplinary Hearing that those staff had received such training from the previous owners; Judge Horne then relied on this to make his decision** *(see 'Image 022b' and 'Image 022c')* – however that was a conscious and deliberate dishonesty as the Fire Risk Assessment Report from Peninsula *(see previous fraud 20)* found that no such training had been done prior to Sept 2014; therefore, when Mr Frodsham put to Claimant at Disciplinary stage, and Peninsula/Employer subsequently put to the Employment Tribunal, that the other Night Staff had done this training under the previous owners, they were fully aware that NO staff had done any such training with the previous owners.

Further, there was no record in the notes of the entire Disciplinary Process *(Investigation, Disciplinary and Appeal)* of Claimant stating to Mr Frodsham that the other Night Staff had received such training from the previous owners; which explains why Judge Horne couldn't determine in which meeting it was supposedly stated. In fact, Claimant is documented as stating that the other Night Staff NEVER had special training with the previous owners *(see 'Image 022d')*, something Claimant would know as FACT because he was their Line Manager and responsible for their training with the previous owners.

Image 022a

"They are appointed persons with specific roles and responsibilities with specific training and skill sets that they had from their previous role as part of ████ and assuming charge when no night managers or supervisors were present as per ████ procedures."

From Judge Horne's written reasons for the Judgment – which was a direct quote from Mr Frodsham as documented in the Disciplinary Meeting Notes 2015. Mr Frodsham tells the Claimant that the other Night Staff had 'specific training' from the previous owners; that's despite Mr Frodsham already being fully aware that NONE of the staff had done 'enhanced training' prior to Sept 2014 and there being no training records from the previous owners.

Image 022b

During the course of the meeting (although it is not entirely clear on which date) the claimant told Mr Frodsham that ████ and ████ had received enhanced fire training prior to the respondent taking over the hotel.

From Judge Horne's written reasons for the Judgment. The reason it was 'not entirely clear' to Judge Horne on which date the Claimant told Mr Frodsham that the other Night Staff had received the enhanced training is because, the

Claimant NEVER made any such statement to Mr Frodsham. The previous 'Image 020a' confirms that it was the other way around; it was in fact Mr Frodsham who told the Claimant that the other Night Staff had done 'specific training' with the previous owners.

Image 022c

> He was aware that ▮▮▮ and ▮▮▮ had had the additional training because he had been present when some of it was delivered and because the claimant had informed him during one of the meetings that they had attended such training.

From Judge Horne's written reasons for the Judgment – Judge Horne relied on the false information from Employer that Claimant had told Mr Frodsham the other Night Staff had done enhanced training.

Image 022d

> JB stated: ▮▮▮ was F&B and that he was moved over and ▮▮▮ had only been at the hotel a few months. Both never had special training and had never been management

From Disciplinary Meeting Notes 2015, which Judge Horne read – Claimant clearly states that the other Night Staff 'NEVER had special training'.

23. **Employer put to Employment Tribunal, or inferred, that ONLY certain staff were trained on the Fire Alarm Panel; Judge Horne confirmed this in his written reasons** *(see 'Image 023a')* – however that was a conscious and deliberate dishonesty because, when Claimant raised this very issue during his Appeal Hearing in 2015, Mr Krohn stopped that conversation dead in its tracks by categorically stating that Fire Alarm Panel Training was passed on to *'ALL'* staff *(see 'Image 023b')*.

Mr Krohn's statement was overlooked at Employment

Tribunal but is very relevant because the Employer elaborated on the Fire Alarm Panel Training by putting to Judge Horne that it was ONLY given to those staff who *'KNEW how to organise a fire evacuation'*, as confirmed by Judge Horne in his written *reasons (see 'Image 023c')*; this now demonstrates that the cover staff left on site by the Claimant must have known *'how to organise a fire evacuation'* because, according to Mr Krohn, Fire Alarm Panel Training was passed on to *'ALL'* staff.

Image 023a

A separate-cohort-of employees-received additional-fire-safety-training.-This included how to organise a fire evacuation and how to operate the fire panel.

From Judge Horne's written reasons for the Judgment – Judge Horne confirms Employer's verbal statement at Tribunal that only certain staff were trained on the Fire Alarm Panel.

Image 023b

KK: We had a full reset and add on in line with IHG requirements, hentland out service contractor did a full training session and this was passed on to all staff including yourself.

From Appeal Meeting Notes 2015 – during Appeal Hearing Claimant wanted to discuss the Fire Alarm Panel because he had not been trained on it and believed that none of the staff were trained on it; Mr Krohn killed that discussion immediately by stating training on the Fire Alarm Panel was passed on to ALL staff including the Claimant.

Image 023c

There was nothing especially complicated about the fire panel, but the respondent reasonably took the view that the only people to be trained in its use were those who knew how to organise a fire evacuation.

From Judge Horne's written reasons for the Judgment – Judge Horne confirms Employer's verbal statement at Tribunal that only staff who KNEW how to 'organise a Fire Evacuation' were trained on the Fire Alarm Panel. However, everyone, including Judge Horne, overlooked Mr Krohn's written statement from the Appeal Hearing; on that occasion Mr Krohn had stated that 'ALL' staff were trained on the Fire Alarm Panel. That now demonstrated ALL staff must have been able to 'organise a fire evacuation'.

24. **Employer put to Employment Tribunal, or inferred, that the Chef was NOT a** *'Responsible Person'* **therefore Claimant should not have left the Chef in charge** – however, as demonstrated by Employer's own actions, that was a conscious and deliberate dishonesty as Employer regularly left the Chef in sole charge of the kitchen, without any Manager being responsible for him, as they had done the morning of 02 Jan 2015 *(see 'Image 024')*, which is the most dangerous place in the hotel as it deals with open gas, naked flames, and food hygiene; the slightest mistake with any one of those can lead to harm, serious injury or death. Putting the Chef in that role gave the impression of the Chef being a *'Responsible Person'* because the role itself required a *'Responsible Person'* be allocated to it.

Image 024

> It was reasonable for Mr Frodsham to conclude that Mr ▇▇▇ did not have the right level of sound judgment. It would not be reasonable to conclude that the claimant knew of the precise reasons for that fact, but it would be reasonable to conclude that the claimant, not having line management responsibility for Mr ▇▇▇, had taken the risk that Mr ▇▇▇ might not be an appropriate person to cover the hotel. It was an obvious risk bearing in mind he was never on the rota of duty managers.

From Judge Horne's written reasons for the Judgment – confirmation that Claimant did NOT have Line Manager responsibility for the Chef; demonstrating that, on the morning in question, or any time when the senior staff member on site was the Claimant or another GSM, the Chef was solely responsible for himself in the most dangerous part of the hotel.

If Claimant 'took a risk', it was that the person who didn't require a Line Manager on site to oversee them in the most dangerous part of the hotel, might themselves be a 'responsible person'. And let's not forget, Mr Krohn revealed to Peninsula that the Chef was better trained and more suitable than the GSM who THEY left in charge of the hotel on 25 Oct 2014 (see previous fraud 17).

25. **Peninsula/Employer put to Employment Tribunal, or inferred, that it was not the Chef's job to cover reception or to cover for a Guest Service Manager** – however, undisclosed evidence *(see image 025a)* demonstrates that this was a conscious and deliberate dishonesty as Mr Krohn had previously confirmed with Peninsula that the Chef had covered reception for the Early Manager on at least one occasion. While the Chef was not a receptionist or a Manager, he would have to deal with any reception or Manager issues that arose for however long a period the actual Manager was away from reception.

Further, it was an *'Express Condition'* in the Employee Handbook that staff could be asked to cover the roles of other staff, which included Managers *(see 'Image 025b' supported by 'Image 025c')*; hence why the Chef covered for the GSM in this instance. Employer also confirmed at Tribunal that a *'responsible person'* could have covered the Manager absence; the Chef was clearly a *'responsible person'* as Employer left him unmanaged in sole charge of the most dangerous place in the hotel *(as detailed in fraud 24)*.

Image 025a

> Kim Eivind Krohn
>
> James states in one of the documents that ▮▮▮▮ covers breaks on reception during his shift and uses Brilliant – is this true, and if so does he do it in chef uniform? Can you elaborate on this please – a regular occurrence or a one-off, relied on to do a checkout or only in emergency? - Maybe once in an emergency he has stood on the desk whilst the early shift duty manager has had to go to a room to help a guest, the point here is, that a duty manager was always present in the building and he was not left alone. he does not use brilliant though and does not have a log in for the PMS (Brilliant)
>
> 20/03/2015 17:17

Communication between Employer and Peninsula – prior to Appeal outcome. Mr Krohn clearly states the Chef covered reception for a Manager; why the Chef covered reception is irrelevant, the fact the Chef covered reception is very relevant as it demonstrates that the Chef could and DID cover reception and covered for a Manager, and also demonstrates that Peninsula/Employer knowingly gave false information when they told ET that the Chef doesn't cover reception or cover for a GSM.

Image 025b

> *F) JOB FLEXIBILITY*
>
> It is an express condition of employment that you are prepared, whenever necessary, to transfer to alternative departments or duties within our business. During holiday periods, etc. it may be necessary for you to take over some duties normally performed by colleagues. This flexibility is essential for operational efficiency as the type and volume of work is always subject to change.

From Employee Handbook which formed part of ALL staff contracts. It clearly states, as an Express Condition, that staff can be called upon to take over duties 'performed by colleagues'; in fact, it's 'essential for operational efficiency' that they can do this. A 'colleague' includes senior colleagues such as GSMs, all the way up to General Manager (supported by 'Image 025c'), and there is NO stipulation in the 'Express Condition' that excludes the duties of any senior colleagues; this is demonstrated by the fact Employer allowed the other Night Staff, who were not employed as managers, to take over the duties of Claimant when he was off work.

Image 025c

1) Informal complaint

We recognise that complaints of personal harassment, and particularly of sexual harassment, can sometimes be of a sensitive or intimate nature and that it may not be appropriate for you to raise the issue through our normal grievance procedure. In these circumstances you are encouraged to raise such issues with a senior colleague of your choice (whether or not that person has a direct supervisory responsibility for you) as a confidential helper. This person cannot be the General Manager who will be responsible for investigating the matter if it becomes a formal complaint.

From Employee Handbook. While this section deals with complaints, it does demonstrate that a 'colleague' includes senior staff such as those with supervisory responsibility and, the General Manager (N.B. the stipulation regarding the GM in this section is simply because a GM could end up investigating the issue; it's not because the GM isn't a 'colleague').

26. **Peninsula/Employer put to Employment Tribunal, or inferred, that Claimant's stress was his own perception of stress; Judge Horne relied on it being Claimant's *'own perception'* when coming to his decision** *(see image 026a)* – however, undisclosed evidence *(see 'image 026b' to 'Image 026f')* demonstrates that this was a conscious and deliberate dishonesty as both Peninsula and Employer were fully aware that Claimant's stress had been officially diagnosed by his GP and that Claimant's health condition was a potential disability; which now makes Employer's decision to leave

Claimant alone and unsupported, in charge of an occupied hotel, on the night in question a reckless decision as Employer could not have foreseen that Claimant's health condition and/or stress would not impact on any action he may have to take in dealing with issues or emergencies that may arise during his shift.

Image 026a

> Mr Frodsham did not take into account the claimant's perception of stress at work, nor was he invited to do so.

From Judge Horne's written reasons for the Judgment; Peninsula/Employer had convinced ET that Claimant's stress was merely his own perception and that Claimant never raised it during the Disciplinary process; Judge Horne therefore gave Employer leeway for not taking the stress into account without any prompting from Claimant.

Image 026b

> **From:** Reception HIEX Leigh - Sports Village
> **Sent:** 13 December 2014 23:36
> **To:** Charles Brimacombe
> **Subject:** Health Assessment
>
> Hi Charlie
>
> Forgot to mention in my last email regarding my blood pressure;
>
> My doctor is concerned about my health condition and work place stress. She suggested I ask you for an 'Occupational Health Assessment'. She said my health condition could have a substantial and long term adverse effect on my ability to carry out day-to-day activities, and needs to be assessed under the disability procedures.

From an email Claimant sent to Mr Brimacombe on 13 Dec 2014. At this point the Employer was made aware of a 'potential disability'; Claimant even suggests an 'Occupational Health Assessment', therefore Employer lost the 'didn't know/couldn't reasonably have known' part of any defence relating to Claimant's health condition. With this information, Employer ought to have taken Claimant's health condition into account at Disciplinary stage without any prompting from the Claimant to do so.

Image 026c

▉▉▉▉▉▉▉
Advised it is strange that the GP would say someone else would diagnose him as having a disability. Ask him to complete a health questionnaire and then come back to me once they are looking to make the occupational health referral. Establish duty of care - a reasonable, yet strange, request.
15/12/2014 16:32

Communication between Employer and Peninsula, on 15 Dec 2014. Peninsula has now been made aware of a 'potential disability' with Claimant. It has to be noted here that Claimant did NOT request that Employer diagnose him as having a disability; Claimant simply requested to be 'assessed under the disability procedures' (see previous 'Image 026b').

Image 026d

Charles Brimacombe
Want to proceed with health assured referral. Has not completed health questionnaire yet
Speak to Steven Frodsham in Charles' absence tomorrow.
16/12/2014 11:56
▉▉▉▉▉▉▉
Advised to ensure he completes he health questionnaire. Will refer to HRAM to follow occ health process.
16/12/2014 11:56

Communication between Employer and Peninsula, on 16 Dec 2014. Mr Brimacombe informs Peninsula that he wants to proceed with a 'health assured referral'. 'Health Assured' was a triage service operated by Peninsula whereby a member of their clinical team may contact an employee once a referral form has been received, but prior to an appointment with either an Occupational Health Advisor (Nurse) or Physician (Doctor) being made, in order to ensure a referral would be appropriate. This however was an unnecessary step as Claimant's GP had already advised that an Occupational

Health Assessment was required; even so, Claimant was never referred to 'Health Assured' despite Mr Brimacombe wanting to proceed.

Image 026e

> **Charles Brimacombe**
>
> He was given a written warning.
> As a result of that he went off sick and now stating that his blood pressure is high.
> 6 days he was off for.
> He is off for a week now and then asking him to complete a health questionnaire.
> He has said that he may have issues carrying out his job role - he has saying that his GP would class this as a disability.
>
> 16/12/2014 13:51

Communication between Employer and Peninsula, on 16 Dec 2014. Mr Brimacombe reiterates to Peninsula about Claimant's condition being a potential disability; therefore Peninsula was well aware of it and ought to have advised Employer to take Claimant's health condition into account at Disciplinary stage.

Image 026f

> Charles Brimacombe
> Tue 16/12/2014 13:59
> To:
>
>   Steven Frodsham;
>
> Hi
>
> Just spoke to ███ at Peninsula regarding that man !
>
> To fill in the health questionnaire on his return
>
> Have a one to one open meeting / welfare meeting discussing the health issues in the e-mail
>
> After this, document & email ███ back with info – to take the next step ie occupational health, requesting doctors information etc
>
> Stuck until he comes back off holiday – But I will deal with this & keep you guys updated
>
> Charlie

Email from Mr Brimacombe to Mr Frodsham, 16 Dec 2014. Mr Frodsham is now made aware that Claimant has 'health issues' and that the next step will be 'occupational health'; this step is not for minor health issues therefore it is reasonable to believe that Mr Frodsham, who had overall responsibility and a 'Duty of Care' for the Claimant, enquired about the details of Claimant's condition and was made aware of a potential disability.

While Employer had no 'Actual Knowledge' of a disability, because Claimant's condition had not been put to the disability test, they did have knowledge of a potential disability from the moment Claimant first notified Mr Brimacombe he had a medical condition that may be classified as a disability under the Equality Act; which in this instance was 13 Dec 2014, and later confirmed by Mr Brimacombe on 16 Dec 2014. Therefore, until it had been confirmed either way, Employer ought to have treated Claimant as if he had a disability, and taken it into account.

'Image 026f' also reveals Mr Brimacombe's contempt for the Claimant i.e. Mr Brimacombe refers to Claimant as 'that man' rather than by name. We are then supposed to believe that, despite this contempt, and despite Mr Brimacombe falsifying investigation notes, that he was truthful when giving evidence against Claimant at Employment Tribunal.

27. **Peninsula/Employer put to Employment Tribunal, or inferred, that Claimant did not raise his *'Workplace Stress Assessment'* during the Disciplinary Process; Judge Horne relied on Claimant not raising the Workplace Stress Assessment when coming to his decision** *(see previous 'Image 026a')* **– however, undisclosed evidence** *(see 'image 027a')* **demonstrates that this was a conscious and deliberate**

dishonesty as both Peninsula and Employer were fully aware that Claimant DID raise his health condition and the *'Workplace Stress Assessment'* during the Disciplinary Hearing, and that Mr Frodsham failed to respond or get into a discussion about those issues. Instead, Mr Frodsham adjourned the meeting *(see 'Image 027b')*.

Although the Claimant's health condition and the *'Workplace Stress Assessment'* were only raised in relation to Claimant being left alone and in charge on the night of 02 Jan 2015, it is now clear they WERE raised during the Disciplinary Hearing, that their affects WERE plainly stated to Mr Frodsham, that Claimant wanted to discuss them, and that they could be mitigating circumstances; which, had Mr Frodsham engaged with those points, would inevitably have led to discussing Claimant being left alone and in charge on other nights such as the 01 Jan 2015.

Mr Frodsham had Tribunal believing that *'the Disciplinary was to hear mitigation'*; therefore, he couldn't then let Tribunal know that Claimant HAD raised his health condition and the *'Workplace Stress Assessment'* because Mr Frodsham would then have to explain why he failed to take them into account as mitigation when he was supposedly looking for mitigation.

Image 027a

Knowing that I have high blood pressure, and knowing that stress could have an adverse effect on my blood pressure, which in turn will have an effect on my health, an investigation meeting was held at the beginning of my shift, which would obviously raise anxiety levels and cause stress. I am then left on shift, alone, for the night. Is aggravating an employee's condition, and then leaving them to cope with the effects alone, the actions of a responsible employer, especially after said employer has just conducted a 'Workplace Stress assessment' which highlights their failings towards me?

From Claimant's notes which he read out and handed over to

Employer during the 2015 Disciplinary Hearing. Employer did not include any of Claimant's notes in the Court bundle which they prepared for Tribunal; Claimant's notes are simply referred to as numbered statements in the minutes of the Disciplinary Hearing, 'Image 027a' above being part of 'statement's 3 and 4'.

Image 027b

JB then went on to read out statement's 3 and 4 and added that he had said everything he had to say and asked if SF had any questions? SF asked: So you have read out all your notes/statements and this is to find out if there are any mitigating circumstances why you left the hotel SF went on to add: I will need to go through all the information you have given me and then we can arrange to meet back up SF gave JB the opportunity to stay whilst he went through the notes or if he wished to reconvene another day which JB agreed to as he was working nights again tonight and needed to get to bed having worked all night last night.

From the minutes of the Disciplinary Hearing 2015 prior to adjournment. Claimant (JB) is documented as reading out 'statement's 3 and 4'; which included reference to his health condition and the 'Workplace Stress Assessment' (as seen in previous 'Image 027a'). As you can see, Mr Frodsham (SF) does not engage with any of the points Claimant put to him in 'statement's 3 and 4'; Mr Frodsham simply adjourns the meeting in order to 'go through all the information'.

It has to be noted here that, after having 8 days to 'go through all the information', Mr Frodsham does not engage with any of the points from 'statement's 3 and 4' during the reconvened hearing either.

28. **Employer put to Employment Tribunal, or inferred, that *'Health & Safety'* was a genuine concern of theirs, hence the 2015 Disciplinary** – however, as demonstrated by Employer's own actions, that was a conscious and deliberate dishonesty as they held themselves to a much lower standard than

Claimant when it came to *'Health & Safety'* for example:-

I.   Employer chained and padlocked a fire exit shut for 2 days while the hotel was occupied with paying guests *(see 'Image 028a')* which was not only a genuine and serious risk to Health & Safety *(see 'image 028b')*, it was also a breach of Fire Safety Regulations.

II.   Employer regularly left Claimant alone and in charge of an occupied hotel, as they did on 01 Jan 2015, and left him to rely on his own *'common sense'* and to use his own judgment knowing he had a condition that could affect his judgment and ability to make decisions *(as detailed in previous fraud 26)* which, in the event of an emergency, could be the difference between life and death.

III. Employer left a member of staff with a drinking problem *(the Chef, as detailed in fraud 11, item 'iii')* in charge of the most dangerous place in the hotel, the kitchen, with NO Line Manager on site to oversee him and NO process in place to determine if the Chef was sober enough to actually work in the kitchen let alone take charge of it.

IV.   Not only did the Chef have a drinking problem, Mr Frodsham also put in his statement of FACT to the Employment Tribunal that the Chef *'didn't know what to do in case of a fire alarm or fire or any other emergency'*; which may well have supported Mr Frodsham's other statement about the Chef not being trained, but was very damning as it also demonstrated that Employer knowingly took a risk with *'Health & Safety'* each time they left the Chef alone and unmanaged to work with naked flames and open gas when they knew he wouldn't know what to do in case of a fire alarm or fire, and each time Employer left him to work with raw uncooked food when they knew he wouldn't know what to do in *'any other emergency'* such as food poisoning.

V.   Mr Brimacombe admitted to staying overnight in a room that could not be registered on the hotel system *(see 'Image 028c')*, again not only a genuine risk to *'Health & Safety'*, it too was a breach of Fire Safety Regulations.

VI.   Employer admitted to Peninsula that they themselves had put an untrained GSM in charge of the hotel on the morning of 25 Oct 2014 *(as detailed in fraud 17)*. It stands to reason that if Claimant's action of leaving untrained staff in charge on 02 Jan 2015 was a risk to *'Health & Safety'*, then Employer's action of leaving untrained staff in charge on 25 Oct 2014 must also have been a risk to *'Health & Safety'*.

VII.   Mr Frodsham, the person who was so concerned about *'Health & Safety'* being put at risk when Claimant left untrained staff in charge on 02 Jan 2015 that he ordered an immediate investigation, admitted that when he started at the hotel in July 2014 he read through ALL employee records *(see 'Image 028d')*; therefore, he would have noticed the lack of *'advanced fire safety training'* (as

119

detailed in previous fraud 20) yet, he had so little concern for risk to *'Health & Safety'* that he didn't have his staff immediately trained or bring in fully trained people until his staff were trained.

VIII. And, as demonstrated in fraud 11, item *'v'*, the Employer had absolutely NO concern in putting the *'Health & Safety'* of children at risk when they publically posted the images of said children on Facebook in breach of Data Protection.

'Health & Safety' was NOT a genuine concern for the Employer; any concern held by Employer about *'Health & Safety'* relating to Claimant's actions was superficial in order to use the *'Health & Safety'* argument as a tool to sanction the Claimant.

Image 028a

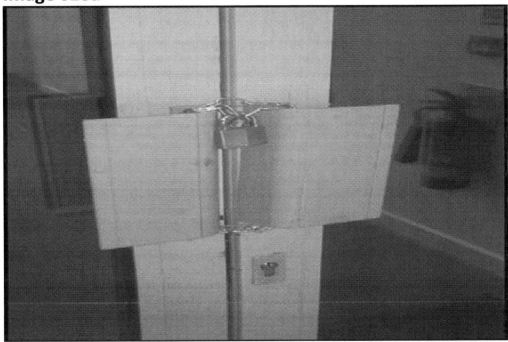

Picture taken by Claimant of the chained and padlocked fire doors – during the 2015 Disciplinary process: this same exit

was identified in a 'Fire Risk Assessment' report by Peninsula in Sept 2014 as being 'found in disrepair, must be repaired urgently'. Employer put to Employment Tribunal that the issue of the fire doors was Claimant's attempt to 'detract away from the seriousness of his own actions'; when in fact, the issue of the fire doors was Claimant demonstrating that Employer had no problem with putting 'Health & Safety' at risk themselves, and that 'Health & Safety' only became an issue when Employer needed to justify their actions against Claimant.

Chaining and padlocking a Fire Exit WAS an actual RISK to 'Health & Safety' because it caused an obstruction to a fire escape route that WOULD prevent guests/staff from escaping in the event of a fire; unlike the hypothetical 'risk' which Employer sanctioned Claimant for.

Image 028b

> Yes this is a prosecution if the fire service inspect and it may not be just senior management who are in the firing line, but the responsible person on the day.
>
> You don't get much more serious than padlocked fire exits!!

Statement obtained by Claimant from an Ex Fire Station Commander regarding the chaining and padlocking of fire exits. Employer was given a copy of this statement during Claimant's Disciplinary process so were fully aware of how serious THEIR own actions were. Employer simply brushed aside their own actions while at the same time they threw the book at Claimant for far less serious actions.

Employer was tasked with preparing the bundle for Employment Tribunal but failed to include a copy of the Ex Fire Station Commander's statement with the Disciplinary notes.

121

Image 028c

> There is a dispute that has taken on a particular significance in this case as to what conclusions can be drawn from a guest ledger that was disclosed for the first time this morning. The evidence of the respondent is somewhat contradictory as to what this tends to show. However, I am quite satisfied that the particular date that this shows, which is the night of 4 January going onto 5 January, on that night Mr Brimacombe was in fact sleeping overnight on the premises in a room that was not sellable and was not included on this particular ledger.

From Judge Horne's written reasons for the Judgment. Employment Tribunal had been given an official hotel 'Guest Ledger' that contained the names of every person in every occupied room for the night of 04 Jan 2015; Mr Brimacombe was not included on the ledger which meant he was not registered on the hotel system and would subsequently not show up on ANY report as occupying a room.

It WAS a legal requirement for all occupied rooms to be registered on the system because, in a fire emergency situation, the information is automatically duplicated onto an Emergency Guest List that allows the Fire Service to know which rooms to concentrate their search efforts on if anyone is missing. For all intents and purposes, Mr Brimacombe was NOT in the hotel that night.

At Employment Tribunal, in order to counter the documented evidence, Mr Brimacombe put forward the narrative that he was at work on 04 Jan and stayed overnight until the morning of 05 Jan in a room that wasn't sellable and could therefore not be registered as occupied on the system. Judge Horne took Mr Brimacombe's narrative over the documented evidence but, in doing so, Judge Horne accepted that Mr Brimacombe was staying in a room that was not registered as occupied on the hotel system. Regardless of the reason given for staying in that room, or the reason given as to why it could not be registered on the system, the fact still remains it WAS a breach of Fire Safety Regulations for Mr Brimacombe to be there. ANY breach of those regulations puts 'Health & Safety' at genuine risk; and now we have Mr Brimacombe admitting in Court that he breached 'Fire Safety Regulations' the night of 04 Jan 2015.

Mr Brimacombe's admission solved one issue for the Employer at Tribunal i.e. it now placed a Manager on site with the other Night Staff on the night of 04 Jan 2015; however, it created other issues which were not addressed at Tribunal i.e. Mr Brimacombe breaching Fire Safety Regulations thereby putting Health & Safety at actual risk, Employer endorsing Mr Brimacombe's risk to Health & Safety by allowing him to stay in a room that could not be registered on the system, and Employer throwing the book at Claimant for allegedly putting Health & Safety at risk while at same time allowing Mr Brimacombe to put Health & Safety at actual risk.

Claimant's actions did NOT breach 'Health & Safety' policy or procedures, and did NOT breach 'Fire Safety Regulations', yet Claimant was investigated the very same day and sanctioned for his actions; which demonstrates that Claimant WAS being treated differently to Mr Brimacombe.

Image 028d

> 15. The outgoing contractor didn't provide any summary information about the staff, but the personnel files were left in the office. When I started, I read through them all.

From Mr Frodsham's written statement of FACT to the Employment Tribunal. As you can see, he clearly admits to reading ALL staff personnel files when he started; therefore, he was fully aware at the beginning of July 2014 that NONE of the files contained any record of staff completing 'advanced fire safety training'.

29. **Peninsula/Employer put to Employment Tribunal, or inferred, that Mr Frodsham was employed by the Employer, KS Hotels Ltd,** *(see 'Image 029')* – however, that was a conscious and deliberate dishonesty as both Peninsula and Employer were fully aware that Mr Frodsham was actually employed by *'Capital Climb Ltd'*, a completely separate company to KS hotels Ltd and unrelated to IHG. Mr Frodsham was in the position of Deputy General Manager at a *'Capital Climb Ltd'* hotel and was brought into the Employer's hotel in July 2014 by Mr Krohn to act as temporary General Manager after the sudden resignation of the existing GM.

At no point was Mr Frodsham employed by the Employer; he was always employed by *'Capital Climb Ltd'* up to and including the day Claimant was dismissed. Peninsula and Employer were fully aware of this when they put Mr Frodsham's statement to the ET.

This now demonstrated that the person hearing a Disciplinary and issuing a sanction did NOT have to be employed by the Employer, did NOT have to be employed by IHG, and did NOT have to be an existing General Manager elsewhere; which greatly opened up Employer's available resources for the Disciplinary Process as they were not limited to only using people from within KS Hotels or IHG, or limited to using General Managers. This is now very relevant to fraud 30.

Image 029

WITNESS STATEMENT: STEVEN FRODSHAM

My name is Steven Frodsham and I will say as follows:

1. I am employed by KS Hotels Ltd and work at Holiday Inn Express Leigh, which is based at the following address: Holiday Inn Express Leigh, Leigh Sports village, Sale Way, Leigh, WN7 4JY.

From Mr Frodsham's written statement of 'FACT' to the Employment Tribunal. As you can see, the very first thing Mr Frodsham states is that he is 'employed by KS Hotels Ltd'.

30. Peninsula/Employer put to Employment Tribunal, or inferred, that being a small business the Employer had limited resources to deal with the Disciplinary process i.e. they only had three people to deal with the process, one person for each stage *(investigation, disciplinary, appeal)*; this caused Judge Horne to give Employer leeway on issues that a larger company would not have been afforded *(see 'Image 030a' to 'Image 030d)* – however, that was a conscious and deliberate dishonesty as previously demonstrated in fraud 29 i.e. Employer had the option of bringing someone in from outside their company to hear Disciplinaries; in fact, it was a *'reserved right'* that Employer could bring in 3rd parties to chair Disciplinary and Appeal Hearings *(see 'Image 030e' and 'Image 030f')*.

Employer also had at its disposal the HR facilities of two multi-million pound global companies i.e. Employer had a contract with Peninsula that included access to their HR people, and Employer had a franchise agreement which meant they were now part of the InterContinental Hotels

Group that allowed Employer access to even more highly experienced HR people. Both Peninsula and InterContinental Hotels Group could, if requested, provide people to chair a Disciplinary or Appeal Hearing.

The fact Employer chose not to use any of the resources available to them is irrelevant; however, the fact those resources WERE available to the Employer is very relevant as it demonstrates that Employer had access to resources equivalent to those of much larger companies which the typical small business didn't have. It also demonstrates that Employer could very easily have allocated truly independent Officers to deal with Claimant, and that they had access to more than enough resources for a proper and fair Disciplinary Process to be conducted in accordance with their own procedures and Employment Law.

Any leeway given by Judge Horne due to Employer being a small business with limited resources was misguidedly given because Employer did NOT have limited resources as they were part of a global hotel group. All leeway given caused detriment to the Claimant.

Image 030a

(4) Where the employer has fulfilled the requirements of subsection (1), the determination of the question whether the dismissal is fair or unfair (having regard to the reason shown by the employer)-
(a) depends on whether in the circumstances (including the size and administrative resources of the employer's undertaking) the employer acted reasonably or unreasonably in treating it as a sufficient reason for dismissing the employee, and
(b) shall be determined in accordance with equity and the substantial merits of the case.

From Judge Horne's written reasons for the Judgment. As you can see, Judge Horne took into account 'size and administrative resources' of the Employer; or what he believed them to be.

Image 030b

> Mr Frodsham chairing the disciplinary meeting. Mr Frodsham's involvement was imperfect. He had witnessed some events that had a bearing on the eventual decision. In particular, he drew upon his own recollection that he had attempted to telephone the hotel and the call had twice rung out. He also took into account his own knowledge of staff training when distinguishing between the claimant's case and that of ███ and ███. That said, Mr Frodsham's involvement was still well within the reasonable range of procedures for this respondent. It is a small organisation and it had little room for manoeuvre.

From Judge Horne's written reasons for the Judgment. Judge Horne identifies a 'conflict of interests' that demonstrates Mr Frodsham could not be independent i.e. Mr Frodsham was a witness against Claimant at the same time he was hearing the Disciplinary against Claimant.

This 'conflict of interests' would not have been accepted as reasonable from a larger company due to their available resources; they would have been expected to get someone else to hear the Disciplinary, especially if the employee concerned had requested the allotted Disciplinary Officer be replaced due to a 'conflict of interests', as was the case in this instance. But leeway was given to 'this respondent' because Judge Horne believed they 'had little room for manoeuvre' i.e. no resources available in order for someone else to hear the Disciplinary.

Image 030c

> Realistically, the only alternative person with authority to discipline the claimant would have been Mr Crohn. That would only have left Mr Briggs to hear the appeal. It was not put to any of the respondent's witnesses that Mr Briggs should have been designated to hear the appeal, and very probably that omission was deliberate and well chosen. Mr Briggs did not take an active role in the operation of the business.

From Judge Horne's written reasons for the Judgment. Because Judge Horne was led to believe there were ONLY three people to deal with the Disciplinary Process, he relied

127

on that to justify the leeway given to Mr Frodsham i.e. Judge Horne believed that if Mr Frodsham had been replaced, the only other person available to hear the Disciplinary was Mr Krohn; but then no one would be left to hear an Appeal.

It has to be noted here that Mr Krohn confirmed in his statement of 'FACT' to the ET, which Judge Horne relied on in 'Image 030c' above, that Mr Briggs the second director 'doesn't take an active role in the operations of the business' i.e. he was a silent partner. Claimant was never aware of Mr Briggs until the Employment Tribunal therefore, realistically, Claimant wouldn't have been able to 'put to any of the respondent's witnesses' that Mr Briggs 'should have been designated to hear the appeal'.

Image 030d

> Mr Crohn's treatment of the appeal did not amount to a full re-hearing, as the disciplinary procedure prescribed. Taken together with the disciplinary meeting, however, it did not bring the investigation outside of the reasonable range for a small employer.

From Judge Horne's written reasons for the Judgment. Judge Horne confirms that the Appeal hearing was not conducted as prescribed by Disciplinary Procedures; not only was this a procedural defect, it was also a breach of Claimant's employment contract as disciplinary procedures formed part of that contract.

Again, this would not be accepted as reasonable from a larger company, but leeway is given to Employer because of the belief that, as a 'small employer', they had limited resources.

Image 030e

> 5) We reserve the right to allow third parties to chair any formal hearing.

From the Employee Handbook – section 'DISCIPLINARY PROCEDURES', subsection 'I) GENERAL NOTES', regarding the Disciplinary Hearing.

Image 030f

> 7) We reserve the right to allow third parties to chair any formal hearing.

From the Employee Handbook – section 'CAPABILITY/DISCIPLINARY APPEAL PROCEDURE', regarding the Appeal Hearing.

31. **Peninsula/Employer put to Employment Tribunal, or inferred, that the new written brand standards that came with the IHG Franchise Agreement did NOT form any part of their reasoning in the subsequent disciplinary action, which was reiterated by Judge Horne** *(see 'Image 031a')***; this was to negate the fact that there was an unresolved dispute as to whether Claimant had been told of specific brand standards** *(see "Image 031b)* **and, because Employer failed to bring those brand standards to Claimant's attention during the Disciplinary Process in order to give him a fair chance to meet the argument before dismissal –** however, that was a conscious and deliberate dishonesty as demonstrated in *'Image 031c'* when Mr Frodsham relied on specific IHG procedures regarding Guest Service Managers to escalate the issue to a Disciplinary Hearing.

Having Managers on site at all times was not a legal requirement, nor was it a requirement of the previous owners, nor was it a requirement of the Employer prior to the franchise agreement. The requirement to have Managers on site at ALL times was solely an IHG requirement and part of the new Brand Standards that came with the IHG Franchise Agreement as demonstrated in previous fraud 18 when Peninsula confirm that Claimant wouldn't have seen a document that stated when GSMs had to be on site, GSM being an IHG designation; and by the fact that the only document submitted as evidence by Employer to the Employment Tribunal regarding Managers having to be on site at all times was an IHG document.

Reliance on the new written brand standards was also demonstrated in previous fraud 21 when *'advanced fire safety'* training was the basis Employer used to determine that a fire evacuation would not run efficiently with the cover staff left in place by Claimant. *'Advanced fire safety'* training was not a legal requirement, nor was it a requirement of the previous owners, nor was it a requirement of the Employer prior to the franchise agreement; *'Advanced fire safety'* training was solely an IHG requirement and part of the new standards that came with the IHG Franchise Agreement as demonstrated in fraud 21 by the fact that no one had done the advanced training prior to Sept 2014, and by the fact that ALL *'GSMs'* were supposed to have done the *'Advanced fire safety'* training before Oct 2014 so they could be left in charge after the hotel was rebranded to an IHG property *(we now know that part was false as Employer admitted to Peninsula that one GSM was NOT trained when she was left in charge on 25 Oct 2014)*.

Further, *'advanced first aid'* training was not a legal requirement, nor was it a requirement of the previous owners, nor was it a requirement of the Employer prior to the franchise agreement. *'Advanced first aid'* training was solely an IHG requirement and part of the new standards that came with the IHG Franchise Agreement as demonstrated by the fact Mr Frodsham stated at Employment Tribunal that he received an email from IHG stating that a set number of First Aiders HAD to be on site, which was referred to by Judge Horne in his written Judgment *(see 'Image 031d').*

The new written brand standards that came with the IHG Franchise Agreement clearly formed part of Employer's reasoning in the subsequent disciplinary action; therefore Claimant was not given a fair opportunity to meet the arguments relating to the new written brand standards before being dismissed.

The unresolved dispute as to whether Claimant had been told of specific brand standards was now very relevant because it was the difference between Claimant knowing and not knowing that advanced training was a requirement of the franchise agreement. The dispute ought to have been resolve before the Employment Tribunal made their judgment; it likely would have been resolved if Peninsula/Employer had not convinced Judge Horne that the new written brand standards did NOT form <u>any part</u> of their reasoning in the disciplinary action.

Image 031a

> With the new franchise also came a new set of written brand standards. These were not drawn to the claimant's attention and did not form any part of the reasoning in the subsequent disciplinary action.

From Judge Horne's written reasons for the Judgment. Managers actually being on site prior to the Franchise Agreement coming into force, or prior to TUPE, does NOT demonstrate a requirement that they had to be on site at ALL times; having written procedures in place would demonstrate such a requirement.

Employer had NO written procedures in place regarding this issue until the IHG Franchise Agreement came into force; therefore the requirement to have managers on site at ALL times was solely an IHG requirement and demonstrates that the new written brand standards that came with the IHG Franchise Agreement DID form part of Employer's reasoning in the subsequent disciplinary action.

Image 031b

In October 2014 the hotel re-opened as a Holiday Inn Express, a franchise granted by IHG. A two day training course was provided to familiarise staff with the brand. There is a dispute as to whether, during this two day training course, the trainees were specifically told that one of the brand standards of Holiday Inn Express was for there to be a Duty Manager present in the building at all times. I have not found it necessary to resolve this dispute.

From Judge Horne's written reasons for the Judgment. Judge Horne acknowledges a dispute but does NOT resolve it because Employer claimed the new IHG Brand Standards 'did not form ANY part of the reasoning in the subsequent disciplinary action'.

Image 031c

Company procedures state there has to be a guest services manager on every shift, so he should have contacted. He assumed that Steve would be in, but that was not until 9 leaving the hotel understaffed/managed. Steve saw the email at 0756, he called his mobile he felt it was answered, employee stated that his batery was flat.

Dear Steven

Please find attached the invite to disciplinary which you should complete and return for approval before sending. The allegation should be:

It is alleged that on 2nd January you left the hotel with insufficient management cover by your failure to take appropriate action in regards to staff sickness, which put the health and safety of guests and the running of the hotel at risk.

03/01/2015 11:35

Communication between Employer (Mr Frodsham) and

Peninsula on 03 Jan 2015 – prior to the Disciplinary Hearing. It clearly states 'there has to be a guest services manager on every shift'. GSM is an IHG designation, NOT a KS Hotels designation prior to the rebrand; therefore, Mr Frodsham had IHG procedures in mind when he escalated the issue to a Disciplinary Hearing.

Image 031d

> In addition, a cohort of employees received advanced first aid training. There was a requirement for a specified number of employees within the organisation to have this advanced training. There was, however, no system in place for ensuring that a person with advanced safety training was always present on the premises.

From Judge Horne's written reasons for the Judgment; confirming Employer's claim that there was a requirement for a specified number of staff to have done the 'advanced first aid training'.

Further, the fact that there was 'no system in place for ensuring that a person with advanced safety training was always present on the premises' demonstrates that Employer themselves took a risk with 'Health & Safety' each time they allocated staff on the rota.

Conclusion

The Claimant may have had questions to answer about his conduct in 2014 and 2015, but he was still entitled to a fair hearing which included not being pre-judged, the sanction not being pre-determined and the Disciplinary and Appeal Officers being impartial; all of which were denied to the Claimant in this instance with the approval of Peninsula.

Claimant then misunderstood the Employment Tribunal system; he wrongly believed that, as a Court, the ET was a place where the truth mattered and facts had to be established. Peninsula/Employer better understood the system and knew that lies and deception was the way to win.

We've given you 31 examples, from just ONE case, of Peninsula/Employer putting false information forward as the *'truth'* to an Employment Tribunal. There are more but these ones were key to the issues to be decided at the Employment Tribunal.

Peninsula/Employer had no qualms in withholding evidence, or misleading an Employment Tribunal, in order to secure a judgment in their favour; which in turn denied Claimant the chance of a fair hearing with Judge Horne. The fact that Peninsula/Employer withheld so much relevant evidence, and put so much false information in its place, demonstrates that Peninsula/Employer were guilty of a conscious and deliberate dishonesty in the presentation and pursuit of the defence in Case No. 2405443/2015, *'Mr J Bagnall v KS Hotels Ltd'*, i.e. the judgment WAS obtained by Peninsula's and Employer's fraud.

At the time of publication:

Mr Charles Brimacombe *(Investigation Officer)* was still employed as Deputy General Manager at the Holiday Inn Express Leigh – Sports Village.

Mr Steven Frodsham *(Disciplinary Officer)* was Business Support Manager at KRO Hospitality Ltd *(previously KRO Hotels Ltd)*.

Mr Kim Eivind Krohn *(Appeals Officer)* had resigned as Director of KS Hotels Ltd *(now 'Leigh Hotels Ltd')*, and sits as Director on several other companies including *'KRO Hotels Preston Ltd'*, *'Peter Street Exclusive Development Ltd'*, *'Peter Street Developments Ltd'*, and *'KRO Hospitality Ltd'* *(previously KRO Hotels Ltd)*.

Peninsula Business Services had rebranded to *'Peninsula'* and opened up more offices worldwide.

Afterword

While the Employer has remained silent on this issue, Peninsula has threatened the Claimant with Court action twice, once in April 2018 and once in August 2019, for *'defamation'* due to information in this book being released online and into the public domain. On both occasions Peninsula was told to go ahead with Court action; on both occasions they didn't.

Peninsula are now out of time; meaning we can republish that information in book form without fear of any Court action for *'defamation'*.

Printed in Great Britain
by Amazon

42542010R00077